MW00861780

Endorsements

"Tracy Reynolds offers a fresh perspective on the issue of leading when you're not the one at the top, which is where most of us spend our lives. The ideas are both practical and heartfelt. This book stands out from others on this subject, as it's full of stories, strategies and steps to take to influence from the 'second chair.' You don't have to be a musician to get it. I highly recommend this book."

--Tim Elmore
Founder of GrowingLeaders.com

"In his book, Second Chair Leadership, my close friend Tracy Reynolds captures the team spirit of true leadership. No leader stands alone by himself or herself in championing any noteworthy cause. A true leader is able to serve as a magnet that attracts talented leaders, instills in them his or her vision and molds them into a cohesive unit.

Tracy served faithfully with me for ten years as we planted, built, and grew a great church from 12 to nearly 2,000 worshippers strong. He took copious notes on every sermon I preached. He created a powerful youth ministry and worship ministry and assisted me in every aspect of the church's life.

The famous Russian composer and conductor Anton Rubinstein was asked, 'What is the most important musical instrument in the orchestra?'

He replied, 'Second fiddle. Without it, you have no harmony.'

Not everyone is called to play the melody or sit in the first chair, but everyone can sit in second chair and play harmony."

--Dr. David Cooper
Pastor Mount Paran Church
Atlanta, Ga.

"I begin most of my mornings writing comments to Tracy Reynolds and reading comments from him. Though miles apart, our early thoughts and words draw us together. Thoughts and words can do that.

In Second Chair Leadership, Tracy Reynolds offers his thoughts and words to you, to me, to us. And they draw us all together.

Haven't we all sat in the second chair in some season of our lives? Don't we each have a boss? Whatever our role or title, wherever we serve, someone somewhere is there to guide our journeys. How we respond to those leaders can help us lead well from our chairs of opportunities and responsibilities.

We might not hold a title. We might not be applauded. We might not get recognized. But Tracy—through his lifestyle, his friendship, and his wonderful words in this book—reminds us how to live without titles or applause or recognition.

He reminds us that it is not uncommon for the better players to be hidden lower in the section. He argues that the best first chair leaders realize that none of us are as smart as all of us.

Tracy believes part of the frustration in leading from second chair is the realization that we cannot control many of the issues that contribute to organizational health or dysfunction. He contends that what we can control, however, is our mindset and our attitude.

I hope we allow Tracy's words to lead us into a better life, whatever our role.

I thank Tracy for living that way. I thank him for writing this book. I thank him for being my friend."

--Chris Maxwell
Author, Pastor, Friend

"The rarest words are those that have come evenly from someone's mind, their heart, and their life's work. Here is a book full of them. Distilled from decades of academic study, real-world practice, and genuine love for both the craft and for people, this book is a goldmine with life and leadership gemstones bursting from its walls cover to cover. Second Chair Leadership brings salient, inspiring wisdom in generous portion to all who lead from anywhere in an organizational flowchart, but especially to the multitudes of us who do so from somewhere south of the tip-top."

--Jon Campbell, M.Div.
Author of *Room 6060: Of Death and Hope, Of Grief and Joy*

"Tracy Reynolds writes with great compassion and experience. He has a unique view from the second chair, one that sees 'things others don't' so that we are not 'tone deaf to the nuances of attitudes and feelings among the rank and file' within our organizations. Much has been written about leadership, but it is good to read about important perspectives of followership. That said, Tracy aptly points out that 'we all have a sphere of influence' and that we should "steward the leadership influence" entrusted to us. His advice is that regardless of where you are in the hierarchy of an organization, you should add value, take initiative, solve problems, and think of others. Great advice. Great read. Enjoy!"

--Ron White, Ed.D.
President (retired)
Emmanuel College

"I love leadership, and I thoroughly enjoyed reading and learning Second Chair Leadership. As a successful college basketball coach, I can't tell you how many light bulbs went off. My appreciation and understanding of what leadership looks like or should look like from different seats grew immensely. I had instant gratitude for the second chair leaders I have been able to serve with. I also realize where I hadn't thrived in some of those opportunities, but now I can in the future. What a great read for coaches, educators, churches, and businesses. All platforms would run better with more and better second chair leaders."

--TJ Rosene
Head Basketball Coach
Emmanuel College

"I have known Tracy for 15 years and have consistently seen him navigate the often-ambiguous function of second chair leadership in a variety of circumstances. What I've observed in him is a sense of settledness in doggedly pursuing the role he's been assigned while capturing the vision and remaining appropriately deferential to senior leaders. That's a tricky space to lead from, and he does it (and articulates how to do it) exceptionally well.

As a second and third (and fourth) chair leader for most of my career, I have already benefited from the insights he shares in this book."

--JJ Getts
Executive Director of Shared Services
New City Church, Charlotte, NC

"Since the pandemic, so many in my generation, myself included, have pivoted or completely changed career paths. We need this message Tracy brings in *Second Chair Leadership*, that we can have a meaningful impact in our organizations no matter where we find ourselves in the corporate structure. He thoughtfully reminds us that humility can and will fuel our desire to keep learning and keep serving, aiding us in making a genuine difference in our communities."

--Maggie Turner, M.Ed.
Founder & President, Illuminate Justice

"Using his experiences in orchestras and symphonies playing the trumpet, Tracy Reynolds mines the meanings from these experiences to take us on a journey of how to better lead from 'the second chair.' In Greek, an orchestra is the space in a play where dancers and musicians would gather to support the main stage actors. A symphony in Greek is a sense of harmony produced by many instruments. It implies an agreement of sound. In this book, full of rich personal illustrations, Tracy gives leaders and co-laborers insight into how to produce a harmony that brings glory to God and how leaders and co-laborers create spaces where a joyful 'dance' can occur that produces life, influence, and purpose. I highly recommend this book for leaders and co-laborers together."

--Dr. Doug Beacham
General Superintendent
International Pentecostal Holiness Church

"For the past 20+ years, I have had the remarkable privilege of watching Tracy Reynolds lead with organizational clarity, passion, and mission from 'the second chair.' The principles and values that Tracy shares in this timely leadership book are more than helpful suggestions; they are the practice of his life. This is a must-read, not just for those serving in the second chair but for those of us who are called to the first chair. First chair leaders need to know, or at least be reminded, of the unique challenges, calling, and giftings of those who faithfully serve from the second chair and their immeasurable value to the health and success of our organizations."

--Tony Vismor
Lead Pastor
Grace Fellowship Church

"Dr. Tracy Reynolds' book, Second Chair Leadership, is powerful. I know the writer and have seen him in action. This book IS his life. It's a perfect volume for all leaders, whatever roles they play, and a must-read for leaders who desire to maximize their influence and make an eternal difference as they honor God and invest in others. I love this book."

--Dr. Doug Carter
Senior Vice President
EQUIP Leadership, Inc.

"Lots of people today enjoy titles, positions, visibility, and seniority--and they think that's what leadership is about. But we know that Jesus Christ taught us differently. He said if we want to be leaders, we must be willing to be invisible and secondary. We must be servants. Tracy Reynolds unpacks that principle in a masterful way in Second Chair Leadership. If you have ever been second-in-command or if you simply want to learn what is required to be a true team player, this book is an exceptional resource. I have watched Tracy Reynolds quietly influence people from the second chair, both in his role at his church and at the Bible college he taught at for many years. Tracy uses valuable lessons from his own experience to help us all learn to lead with humility."

--J. Lee Grady
Director, The Mordecai Project
Author, *10 Lies Men Believe* and *Follow Me*

"In an era obsessed with achievement and 'making it to the top,' Tracy Reynolds offers a refreshing vision of leading from 'second chair.' This book explores the biblical pattern of honoring those over us while helping readers see the wisdom and insight that can only come from the vantage point of leading from the middle. As Reynolds notes, this middle space is where most of us spend our lives. What if we did so with glad awareness of how success in the body of Christ is not a matter of being in a top position but a matter of serving in a place fit for our unique gifts? I dare say, this awareness would curb a great deal of fear and anxiety rampant among ministers today. Read this unique book and find a way out of the anxiety-producing, competitive world of current leadership studies."

--Cheryl Bridges Johns
Visiting Professor/Director of Global Pentecostal House of Study
United Theological Seminary

SECOND CHAIR LEADERSHIP

ONLINE RESOURCES

Scan the FlowCode below to access exclusive online resources at

https://www.ctracyreynolds.com/

SECOND CHAIR

LEADERSHIP

HOW TO SERVE, THRIVE, & LEAD

FROM WHERE YOU PLAY

DR. C. TRACY REYNOLDS

Second Chair Leadership

How To Serve, Thrive, & Lead From Where You Play

Copyright © 2023 by Dr. C. Tracy Reynolds

All Scripture quotations are taken from the Holy Bible, New International Version®, NIV®. Copyright ©1973, 1978, 1984, 2011 by Biblica, Inc.™ Used by permission of Zondervan. All rights reserved worldwide. www.zondervan.com The "NIV" and "New International Version" are trademarks registered in the United States Patent and Trademark Office by Biblica, Inc.

True Potential, Inc.
PO Box 904, Travelers Rest, SC 29690
www.truepotentialmedia.com

ISBN: 9781960024084
ISBN: 9781960024091 ebook
LCCN: 2023941119

Printed in the United States of America.

Cover Design: Cindy Reynolds
Author Photo: Justin Reynolds

Contents

Acknowledgments

I have put this off as long as I can, not because I am ungrateful but because I have a real fear of leaving anyone out. When you have lived for nearly two-thirds of a century, you have two things working against you – an endless list of people to whom thanks are due and an ever-decreasing capacity to remember to include them! But here goes...

I am grateful to every first chair leader who ever gave me a chance to serve in your organization and on your team. From a newspaper route as a preteen to high school summer jobs with textile plants or school maintenance crews, or retail stores, I am grateful for the opportunities to work and learn.

I am forever indebted to the band directors, piano teachers, trumpet teachers, orchestra conductors, big band leaders, record producers, recording engineers, sound techs, worship leaders, choir directors, and musical colleagues through the decades. These days I am grateful to Big Band Athens, RiffNotes, Xzalt, and Rathaus for saving me a seat in your group.

My senior pastors have been the first chair leaders in my life for over four decades of service in the local church. Many of them are named at various points in this book. None of them are excluded from my heart of deepest thankfulness for their leadership, modeling, and trust. I am deeply thankful for each leader I have served in the church world in America and in countries like Jamaica and the Philippines, in particular.

Emmanuel College has been a large part of my life for over twenty-five years. I never dreamt of serving alongside college presidents, deans, vice presidents, schools of ministry, student life staff, senior leadership teams, faculty, staff, coaches, or higher education student leaders. I am deeply grateful to every person I have been blessed to know and serve together. They literally occupy every imaginable seat in the organization.

My first challenge to write was offered by a seminary professor in Makati, Dr. T, over 20 years ago. It only took me twenty years, but I am grateful that he saw something I did not see. However, my most persistent encourager in writing endeavors is my buddy for life, Chris Maxwell. Thanks for putting up with me all these years while not giving up on me in so many areas of life and leadership. I would never want to do this, nor could I, without you. Terry Ross has been my friend since I was in college. We have walked through every season of life together. I am grateful for every minute I have with you. I am a better man because of your influence and example.

Finally, my family is my heart. I was blessed with amazing grandparents, parents, and the two best brothers on the planet. I have learned more about life and leadership from my parents, siblings, and extended family than from any book or classroom. My wife, Lisa, is my ultimate supporter and soulmate. She is the most amazing second chair leader I have ever known. Thank you for supporting and encouraging me through every season of life. I love you. Lisa and I are blessed beyond measure with our grown children and grandchildren: Justin, Cindy, Jordan, Troy, Nora, Sadie, and Sophie. Grammy and Papa adore you.

Ultimately, Jesus is my leader. He sits in the highest chair of my life. I owe him my life. I will spend eternity saying thanks.

Thank you all so much.

Foreword

If you've ever played musical chairs as a kid, you'll remember that you sometimes find yourself without a chair. That's an awkward feeling, like you're out of place, don't fit, or maybe wonder how to get a chair next time. We can feel something similar when we occupy a chair in an organization that we're not confident about how we fit in or how it all works.

From my 40 years of leading from the second chair, I can tell you that this book will help you gain confidence about the chair you occupy. Second chair isn't second best. It's not about the chair you sit in; it's who sits in the chair. The level of significance your "chair" carries resides in you, not where you sit in the org chart.

There are a few second chair seats that may carry more influence, such as executive pastor, vice-president, or dean, but the truth is that other than the senior pastor, CEO, or president, etc., we all sit in second chairs of some kind, and your influence is greater than you think. This book is about learning to lead with a servant heart from whatever chair you sit in.

The significance of your role and responsibility is easy to see. Think of it this way. The first chair leader is one person. No matter how gifted he or she is, first chair is one leader. Everyone else forms a team that can become a mighty force for good. It might be three, thirty, or three hundred on the team, yet the magnitude of that leadership is immeasurable. And you have the privilege to help lead the way.

The better you know how to work and lead in harmony as a unified team, for the progress of the vision and the good of the people, the more lives you get to impact in a positive way.

Leading from the second chair is more art than science. Most of us start out with more questions than answers. Questions such as:

- Where do I fit?
- When do I lead and when do I follow?
- How much authority do I have?
- Who speaks up for me?
- How many bosses do I have?
- Is it OK to aspire to another chair?
- What is the best way to lead in my role?

Even if you are "*the*" second chair, these questions are still relevant, with just a slightly different context.

Second chair leadership can be challenging at times. The primary reason is that you are simultaneously leading in multiple directions. You lead up, down, and across. You are side by side with differing voices, opinions, and amounts of influence. And you, like the others, have your own pressures to deal with as you endeavor to solve problems. Welcome to leadership in the second chair. I'll let you in on a little secret, when you understand how all this works, when you know who you are and lead from self-awareness, you can truly lead with joy and a deep sense of meaning and purpose.

You may be called to lead from the first chair in the future, and if so, that's great. But don't miss the joy, short-change your learning opportunities, or lessen your current productivity because you were so focused on the chair "above" you that you didn't fully live and lead in the present. That's a common mistake. Fully embrace the role you were selected for, build what you have been entrusted with, and enjoy the journey. Strive to be good where you are rather than striving for your next.

If you already know you possess the heart, desire, wiring, and passion of a second chair leader, that's awesome, it's a privileged role, and the content of this book will help you thrive as you lead. You'll gain wisdom and insight into so many vital areas, such as the artful nuance of relationships, the significance of attitude, the intricacies of authority, common mistakes to watch out for, the importance of character, truth about limitations, the power of expectations, and so much more.

Allow me to share a few axioms I've learned from experience over many years that have served me well as a second chair leader. As you read this book, you'll find practical wisdom to help you put each of them to practice.

1. Environment is more important than position. The organization you're part of is more important than the perfect job.

2. Honesty and trust are the cornerstones of all relationships.

3. Competency will get you in the door; character will keep you there.

4. Authority is always transferred to you; never start thinking you are the source of your authority. Your influence is about stewardship, not power.

5. Always want more for the people you lead than from them.

We know that the content of a book is a reflection of the author who writes it. If you don't know Tracy and one day have the opportunity to share a cup of coffee, take it. You'll feel like you've met a friend for life. My first cup with Tracy was in Kyiv, Ukraine, where we taught leadership together to a hundred or more church leaders. When you travel with someone to a foreign country, teach through translators, eat unfamiliar food – (not exactly sure what it is), and all the while you're slightly sleep deprived, the real "you" comes out. *That* Tracy has the heart of a shepherd and the mind of a leader with decades of experience in second chair roles. Underneath that is a character that reveals the traits of humility, kindness, and wisdom. That's the birthplace of this book.

Second Chair Leadership takes a refreshing and uplifting approach with a warm and inviting style. So, pour a cup of coffee, drink in some wisdom, and grow as a leader while you move through the pages of this book and put the principles to practice.

Dan Reiland,
Executive Pastor
12StoneChurch

Introduction

Arriving first, being first, striving for first place, and sitting on top of the heap have been the mode of operation for most of us in the Western world. Nobody shoots for second-best in life. Not when first is an option. I've never met an athlete whose goal for the game, race, or season was to come in second place. Yet there are far fewer openings for that position in the league standings or on the organizational chart. There can only be so many senior executives, presidents, head coaches, lead pastors, kings, queens, five-star generals, or governors. There are only so many C-suites and prime parking spaces available. The hard truth is that most of us will live our lives from at least second chair or even lower...much lower...in the grand scheme of things. I think that is something to be celebrated and leveraged for the greater good.

As a follower of Jesus, I am discovering this is normative and to be desired. Jesus warned us to steer clear of the kinds of leadership that celebrate being the boss over others. He challenged his closest followers to be different and pursue higher aspirations than power, wealth, and position. We are to live as if we have no one to impress and only one to satisfy.

We are to play for an audience of One.

We should order our lives in such a way that only God receives glory, and we deflect the credit.

Rather than serving ourselves, we should assume responsibility for the care of others and help meet their needs. Ultimately, there is only one true first chair, and it is already taken!

So, if I don't care who gets the credit, what difference does it, or should it make if I ever sit in the driver's seat vocationally or positionally in the organizations I serve? And even if I am one of those privileged few who get to warm a first chair seat, how might I treat others differently if I were keenly aware that the first chair really doesn't belong to me? What might happen if we began to fully accept and engage the potential influence of living from second chair?

That is the essence of this book.

Of Chairs and Hierarchies

Structure is a good thing. Organization is also a good thing. Too much of a good thing is not a good thing. Every organization needs to organize to accomplish its mission and achieve its goals. I have always been fascinated by the study of leadership and organizational complexity. Nothing intrigues me more than high-performing cultures, championship teams, impactful ministries, or loosely-knit groups of individuals who play to their given strengths, common good, and benefit of communities. Each of these examples has some type of structure and some level of organization. Somebody is in charge, and everybody has a role. Everyone has limits. Everyone has responsibilities. Accountability is achieved if success is continuously experienced.

For our purposes in this book, I have chosen the language of bands, orchestras, and instrumental ensembles to describe positions of authority in terms of chairs occupied by those within the respective organization. Theirs is a hierarchy of "chairs." Every section has a section leader. They sit in first chair. The flute section has a first chair flutist, the saxophone section has a first chair saxophonist, and so on. Each section typically has subsections as well. It is quite common in bands, orchestras, and jazz big bands for one or more individuals to play different harmonic or melodic parts within the same section. There may be as many as three, four, or five parts within any given section, while other instruments might require fewer subsections.

First chair players play first part, second chair players play second parts, etc. And in larger groups, there may be several different people playing the same parts. In my college marching band, there were twenty or more trumpet players playing first part, but we had one first chair trumpeter. One part is not better or more necessary than the others. Each is important and integrates into the common goal of a well-executed musical performance. Chairs help us aggregate the people within each section. The goal of any good director is to get the right people in the right chairs.

Like positions on an athletic team, each chair requires different skill sets and competencies. Different strokes, different folks. Some chairs require tactical, hands-on, or practical skills, while others incorporate strategic thinking and bigger-picture mindsets. Each chair is interdependent on the other chairs and requires listening, responding, complementary action, and cooperation. Every seat has its unique set of challenges and requires problem-solving at every level.

In musical organizations, it is understood that practice is required of everyone privately so that rehearsals held corporately can achieve the mutually desired level of musical effect, aesthetic appeal, and functional excellence. Everyone has a seed to sow…or a horn to blow. Beautiful music can only be achieved to the extent that every person in every chair does their part on a consistent basis.

If you are following my analogy closely, you may be wondering about even bigger-picture questions.

Who chooses the music for the upcoming concert? How are players chosen and seats assigned? Who makes the decision to fire or disassociate with negligent or careless players? Who promotes, advertises, and sells the tickets for performances? Who sets the salary scale for the players, and what criteria are used to determine each salary? Who books the venues, sets the décor, designs the programs, decides what everyone wears, trains the ushers, collects the tickets, and cleans up when it is all over?

While those are real concerns, they are all questions beyond the scope of this book. Our focus will be on learning to thrive from wherever we sit in the organization we serve. And just in case you are wondering, you do not have to be a musician or have any working knowledge of musical organizations to understand the concepts we will discuss. I promise.

Where You Sit is Where You Stand

My mother worked for the Board of Education for many years. One of her superintendents often used the phrase, "Where you sit is where your stand." Vantage points affect what we see, hear, understand, and how we feel about issues relevant to us. Perspective is situational. You have experienced this if you have ever had nose-bleed seats at a concert or end zone seats at a football game. Your experience, compared to that of someone seated in the center section directly in front of the audio engineers or a fan seated on the first row of the fifty-yard line, is vastly different! Where you sit colors what you see. Awareness of perspective and sharing from the collective can provide a competitive advantage to any organization willing to consider the implications of where you sit. There can be much learned from the perspective of second chair. Ignorance or lack of awareness of perspectival variance can lead to irrelevance or losing touch with the constituency of stakeholders in any organization. It is important that we learn from the points of view represented by all the chairs.

Bloom Where You Are Planted

There is nothing uglier to me than a bitter old man or woman. Don't get me wrong, bitterness and negativity are ugly at any age, but it seems tragic to grow old while complaining, fault-finding, and cursing the day. Admittedly, I am hard-wired for positivity genetically. I cannot help it. I am aware that I can be blind to faults, oblivious to evil intent, and unaware of hidden risks if I am not careful. But what if the first step towards a more fulfilling and meaningful life is accepting where I am? Growing up, I often received the challenge to "bloom where you are planted." Start where you are and go from there. Dad would say, "If life deals you a lemon, make lemonade!" Rather than wishing I was someone else, living somewhere else, or leading from a different chair on the organizational chart, what if I could learn more about the multitude of advantages of my vantage point?

I want to help you with that. It is my hope that you will not only recognize and embrace where you sit but you will take steps to excel and celebrate your seat as well.

The Best Seat in the House

After over four decades of leading from the middle of the pack, I want to make the case that second chair just may be the best seat in the house! Scott Mautz claims, "Those who lead from the middle experience a breadth and depth of scope and roles like no one else in an organization. Revel in the choreographed dance you excel at. Believe that leading effectively from the middle is a craft and that you're on your way to becoming a craft master, something to take pride in. Know that you don't have to be *the* leader to be *a* leader."[1] Second chair leadership matters. Who we are, what we do, and how we do it as second chair leaders may determine the success or failure of

---

1   Scott Mautz, *Leading From the Middle* (Hoboken: John Wiley & Sons, 2021) 24.

our team, our mission, or our longevity. I am inviting you to journey with me through a comprehensive tour of the multifaceted world of leadership from the second chair in the grand hope that you will thrive from wherever you sit in your organization.

SECOND CHAIR

Not the Gig I Signed Up For

This is not the gig I signed up for. Nope, not by a long shot. For those of you not associated with the world of performing arts, a gig is an engagement. Booking agents book gigs. In the broader sense, a gig can be a season of life, a vocational assignment, or an organizational position. Whatever you may call your season or assignment, I can assure you that any resemblance between my career path and the path I envisioned as a high school or college student is strictly coincidental, if not random.

Don't get me wrong. I love my life and my vocation. It's just not what I thought I would do or where I thought I would be as I begin the final third of my life. I am not smart enough to have planned all the twists, turns, curveballs, predicaments, blessings, train wrecks, victories, events, processes, tragedies, and pathways that have converged to bring me and my family to this point at this time.

None of it shocks God, however. I have a hunch God knew all along but played my cards close to His vest. And I have a sneaky suspicion most of you can totally relate!

From Worst to First Chair

I can't remember why I chose to play trumpet when I signed up for fourth-grade band. I wanted to play drums, but I think Dad shot that idea down, citing a neighborhood noise ordinance or something to that effect. But I do remember that I held the honor of sitting thirteenth chair out of thirteen trumpet players. For those of you unfamiliar with the culture of school band programs, it matters where you sit in the respective section of the band. First chair is a spot reserved for the elite, the few, and the best of the best players in that band or ensemble. And, in case you are wondering, thirteenth chair was reserved for the worst player in our trumpet section. That was my chair. Obviously, I was not a natural trumpet virtuoso. I started out the worst.

There is a wonderful mechanism employed by many if not most, bands, orchestras, or choral groups…the challenge. A challenge was the band version of the old-fashioned duel or gunfight scene right out of the old-time Western movies. One person of lower rank would challenge the next person of higher rank to a duel of sorts. This was the method of promotion within the band and gave me my best shot at improving my rank in the trumpet section. Of course, such a challenge is not without the risk of potential humiliation. If you failed in your challenge, you weren't kicked out of band, but you did stay seated in your previously held seat.

Did I mention that I sat thirteenth chair?

So, I guess I really didn't have that much to lose.

I have no idea why I thought it was a good idea, but one day I decided to challenge the kid in twelfth chair. As the challenger, I got to choose the song we would perform in front of our peers the next day. Mama did not raise a complete idiot. I took note that my band director was in his final year before retirement and had previously served a full military career in the United States Marine Corps band. I made the politically correct choice of selecting "The Marines Hymn" as our battle hymn for the challenge.

Not to brag, but I nailed it. My director was so pleased with the way I played it that he allowed me to conduct spontaneous challenges to the next eleven players seated to my left that day, and I nailed it thirteen times. And, as unlikely as it seems, in one day, I moved from thirteenth chair to FIRST chair! From worst to first in a day! If I were inclined to brag, it would be worth noting that it took the Atlanta Braves an entire 1991 baseball season to move from the worst team in the eastern division of the National League to first place. As a fourth grader, I did it in a day. Just sayin'. I think that was the day I decided music just might be a good fit for me. Oorah!

Big Fish, Small Pond

Not all school bands are equal in size or musical prowess. I am from Winder, a small town in north Georgia twenty minutes from Athens, the home of the University of Georgia. Our band was large but only slightly above average in musicality compared to the other high school music programs in our region. When our band director retired, the school system hired Mr. Elliott. With his constant encouragement and tutelage, I retained my first-chair status through fifth grade and all through middle school. In fact, it was my band director, Mr. E, who introduced me to private instruction from a graduate student at the university and later to Mr. Ligotti, the primary trumpet professor at the University of Georgia.

District bands, All-State bands, orchestra, jazz band, band camps, and a summer at Governor's Honors in Music set me on a path playing trumpet that seemed to have the potential for a college scholarship and maybe even a career in music at some level. Mr. E was and is far more than a band director to me and my younger brother, Mitch, who played trombone in the band and probably has more musical talent than I ever had. He was the kind of leader who used vacation days and his own finances to help support my district and state-level trips. We made those trips together, and I learned as much about life and leading as I learned about music. That kind of servant leadership inspires me to this day to become more selfless and sacrificial. More about that later.

Our home church, the Winder First United Methodist Church, had a phenomenal music education program with a graded choir system, a variety of vocal ensembles, and even a brass quintet. Our director, "Miss Beulah" Robinson, mentored me and other students through middle and high school. We were afforded constant opportunities to sing and play in our community at civic organizations and church events. By the time I reached high school, I had taken piano lessons for about six years. While I tolerated the classical pieces I was required to play for recitals, I really loved playing rock and jazz. I quickly learned that re-arranging familiar hymns to contemporary harmonies was particularly fun and pleased my parents.

My parents afforded me countless weekly music lessons and bought me a beautiful professional-grade trumpet. My friends and I formed a couple of rock bands to play parties, clubs, and high school proms. Sometimes I even got paid! Rather than buy a car, I bought keyboards and a Leslie tone cabinet. I was a bit of a trumpet player by day and a keyboard player by night. As a high school freshman, I was chosen to travel to Europe with a choir from the North Georgia Conference of the United Methodist Church to sing and play trumpet with the group. I was voted by my senior class "Most

Talented" and was band captain during my senior year. Music was my thing. I was a big fish in a small pond. And, more than I was aware at the time, music was too closely tied to my identity.

A Dime a Dozen

After I graduated high school, I decided to attend the University of Georgia as a Music Education major with trumpet as my major instrument. Most of my competition as a trumpet player came from the Athens area high schools, and most of us took trumpet lessons from the same teachers. As such, we became friends, and our 'competition' was healthy. It was a bit sobering to discover that good trumpet players were not that hard to find, or as my dad would say, "they are a dime a dozen!" Elite players are fewer and far between, however. A small handful of my classmates at UGA would go on to graduate programs and professional careers as performing artists.

My parents had wisely counseled me to consider a degree in music education so that I would have a career option as a teacher as a failsafe should a vocation in music not be viable for me. As is true in most fields, profoundly gifted individuals rise to the top and occupy the first chair positions in the music business. My friend, Phil Clark, was one of those elite individuals who combined hard work, deep passion, and innate musical capacity to secure lifelong careers in the music business. While I was among the best in my class, I was clearly not the best. And during my college years, my life priorities significantly shifted such that music no longer occupied the highest place, and my destiny in music began to change over time.

Changing Identities—Then Along Came Jesus and Frank

Church was a key part of my life growing up. My grandfather was the custodian at the church we attended, and often, during our weekly sleepovers at my grandparents' home, we would help with his duties around the church. From cutting grass, buffing floors, polishing brass, stacking chairs, trimming hedges, cleaning up after weddings, or changing lights in the crawl space above the sanctuary ceiling, my two brothers and I were afforded a perspective of service rarely seen among the average church attenders. Grandaddy Stewart was a servant who never really saw himself as a leader. But much of what I have learned about servant leadership was caught from my observations of him as he served faithfully as the custodian at Winder First United Methodist Church.

My brothers and I attended church with our parents and grandparents from conception through young adulthood. We were surrounded by beautiful examples of Christlikeness in our family and extended family. We were equally blessed to have some amazing role models among the Sunday School teachers, volunteers, pastoral staff, and youth pastors. As a senior in high school, my younger brother Mitch and I attended a youth retreat where we both chose to follow Jesus Christ as our Lord and Savior. While I am sure we had both prayed committal prayers at various stages in our development, this retreat began a trajectory of life transformation for me. That Friday night, I opted to accept my youth pastor, Frank Beard's challenge to "commit as much of my life as I could to as much of God as I could

> **I OPTED TO COMMIT AS MUCH OF MY LIFE AS I COULD TO AS MUCH OF GOD AS I COULD UNDERSTAND.**

understand." That prayer resonated with me then and still today as one of the most honest, authentic admissions of our need for right standing with God through Jesus Christ. What I could not know was the impact it would have on my values and, eventually, my vocational journey.

Jesus Changes the Pecking Order

One Sunday early afternoon, I was playing a keyboard at a local restaurant when a young businessman introduced himself, complimented my playing, and gave me a business card with his name, Terry Ross, and the name of the furniture store he managed. Over the next few months, we became close friends. I soon discovered that Terry was an amazing vocalist looking for a way to use his talents in the service of God. Almost as an experiment, we met to try our hand at writing Christian music.

Over the next several years, we wrote over fifty songs, recorded three albums, and wrote an Easter musical premiered by our local church choir and drama team. We formed a contemporary Christian music band and began traveling on weekends playing worship services, retreats, conferences, and music festivals. Though I was playing trumpet in the UGA Redcoat Marching band and traveling with the football team to the Sugar Bowl and Cotton Bowl as a freshman and sophomore, I dropped out of the marching band and focused more and more time with Terry and our group, Visions, each weekend.

To be the best at something, you must invest large amounts of time, energy, and effort into it. Talent alone is not sufficient. And sustained hard work, in and of itself, is also not enough. High capacity and hard work couple to provide opportunities for advancement and recognition of achievement. Both require your heart to be completely in your work. There must be a "love for the game" that supersedes rigor, discipline, drill, practice, and repetition.

Somewhere between my freshman and junior years at college, my heart changed. Music was no longer at the top of my priorities. While I continued to love learning, playing, and honing the craft, music no longer defined me as a person. I had become a follower of Jesus and was learning to give Him first place and the primary consideration in all my decisions. I realize now that it showed up in my trumpet playing as my heart was becoming less and less engaged, and my commitment to the craft of playing a horn diminished. I would go on to get married after graduating with my music education degree and spend the first year of our marriage on the road with our Christian band, Visions.

God had turned my life and priorities upside down.

People were more important than music to me.

And I almost never thought about the order of the chairs around me or which seat I currently occupied. What may have looked like drift on the outside was direction on the inside.

First Chair No More

First chair had been my seat for most of my middle school and high school career. I sat first chair in the band and even at Governor's Honors in the jazz band. I was in the gifted class. I was band captain. My band director even carved out an internship program during my senior year, where I worked alongside him and was given unofficial leadership and input into the inner workings of the high school band. He even let me arrange "Happy Birthday" for the marching band at the 50th anniversary of my high school homecoming football halftime show. (Yes, I realize it is only 16 measures… but it took me a long time to get it right!)

I was a leader in my church's student ministry all through high school. For three years, I was the co-leader of our youth choir along with my buddy, Wes Kilpatrick. I was co-leader of Visions, the contemporary Christian music group Terry Ross and I formed. First chair seemed like the best spot for me, and there was no indication that would ever change.

I think I believed I would be sitting in first chair all my life. I was wrong. My Mama always challenged us boys to be the best version of ourselves we could possibly be. "Be the best you *you* can be," she would say.

My wife, Lisa, drilled a similar truth into the psyche of our children, Justin and Jordan. She repeatedly instructed them that there would always be someone smarter, better looking, stronger, or faster than you. Don't worry about that. That is not your business or responsibility. You can learn from anybody anywhere, anytime. Learn from them and get better so you can be the best you possible. It has taken me a while to acknowledge and embrace the reality that I am not best suited for first chair leadership. Otherwise, God would have placed me there a long time ago.

From the day I graduated college until this day, I have operated from a second chair leadership position and perspective. In the local church, I have served as Youth Pastor, Worship Pastor, Christian Education Pastor, Assimilation Pastor, Discipleship Pastor, and most currently serve as Campus Pastor for a small church plant thirty minutes away from my home church. During my years serving full-time in higher education, I have been an instructor, Campus Pastor, Dean of the School of Christian Ministries, and Vice President for Student Development.

None of those positions is first chair. After all, the modern world we inhabit—a world that glories in the grind and revels in the influential—has a subtle way of suggesting that significance and worth are about visibility and elevation.

I HAVE LEARNED TO BE OK WITH SECOND CHAIR POSITIONS. MOST DAYS I PREFER IT.

The higher up you are and the more you stand out, the more meaningful your mark on this world will be. Today thankfully, after decades of not being top-dawg, I have learned that this suggested script from an achievement and image-obsessed world is not necessarily true. In that, I have learned to be OK with second chair positions. Most days I prefer it. I have thought about it a lot. I have a huge leadership library and have read a lot of the books in it. I listen to several podcasts every week. Almost all of them are about leadership growth and development or spiritual growth and development. But I sit in second chair and lead from that perspective. Always have. Always will. And I am still learning to lead from second chair.

Personal Reflection and Group Discussion

- Have you personally experienced times or seasons in life that caught you off guard or took you by surprise? How did you feel about it as it was happening?

- As you view your life through the rear-view mirror and assess where you are considering all you have experienced, at what points can you see the hand of God or trace His leading? How has your journey impacted your relationship with God and others?

- Recall any times when you have felt inadequate, unprepared, or un-qualified for the role you were asked to play or the position you were called upon to fill. How did you handle it? What might you change if given the opportunity again?

- Do you find yourself serving mostly in second chair roles or first-chair roles? Do you have a preference? Why or why not? Are there parts of Tracy's story you can relate to or has your experience been different than his?

First Chair Realities and Advantages

Empathy begins with me feeling some portion of your pain in my heart. Feeling the pain of another is not an exact science. Though I feel pain with you, it is not really your pain I feel. I don't really know how you feel, but I care enough to dare enter the arena and share the load you currently carry. So, why include a chapter on first chair leadership realities in a book dedicated to the concept of second chair leadership?

> THE BEST SECOND CHAIR LEADERS LIVE WITH A DEEP SENSE OF EMPATHY FOR FIRST CHAIR LEADERS.

The best second chair leaders live with a deep sense of empathy for first chair leaders. Awareness of the unique perspective and gravity of first chair leadership helps frame a more complementary second chair role and response.

Though I have mostly operated from a second chair perspective, I am aware of certain first chair realities. Like any position, there are advantages and disadvantages. I am sure that my list would differ from a tenured first chair leader's list, but from where I sit, these are some of the realities and advantages. To be fair, we will discuss some of the second chair realities and advantages in the next chapters. In this chapter, we will highlight some of the advantages or perks associated often with leading from the first chair. Some are real, while others are perceived to be real. Because perception can become reality, I feel it is worth our mention in this discussion.

The Buck Stops Here

First chair leaders often have the final authority. Their say is it. And at the end of the day, they are ultimately responsible. The buck stops here. I am keenly aware that everything I get to do as a second chair leader is due to the first chair leader's delegation of authority to me. I feel the weight of that responsibility and highly appreciate the trust of my first chair leader. In my mind, it is up to me to see to it that the job gets done well and in a timely manner.

Authority is a bit of a double-edged sword. If things go well, either people do not notice, or they may be impressed by our good work or excellent service. But if things go poorly or we do not deliver the goods on time, things can end badly for both the first and second chair leaders.

As a leader in the church world, I am also aware of the weight the lead or senior pastor shoulders as the spiritual authority over a church. They answer ultimately to God and, more than likely, to a board of elders who have a variety of expectations regarding what is done and how things are to be done in the church. The stakes are high because the implications could have eternal significance. While God is incredibly full of grace, not everyone on planet Earth is quite so gracious!

The best pastors assume responsibility when things go poorly but share the accolades when things go as planned. I am aware that the senior leader receives many more emails, texts, and phone calls about everything from the controversial teaching content of the student ministries to the unhealthy snacks served in the nurseries. They may never complain, but you can know with assurance that the buck stops with the first chair leader.

People Think You Can Do Anything

Many people who sit in first chair get there because of their competence. Competence is earned by being the best or at least by being the best competitor at auditions, public performances, or in showmanship. However, there are numerous paths one can travel to rise in power or position. In many cases, they have proven themselves in similar positions in other organizations, earned their way up through the ranks of the current organization, or exhibited the desired skills and capacities required for the first chair leadership role. There are outlier examples where the first chair leader inherited the position as the heir to the position due to family ties or outright succession from father to son or mother to daughter. Regardless of how they arrive at the first chair position, trust must be earned and respect gained over time.

There is a very real tendency to assume that, due to their position of responsibility and experience, the first chair leader is competent in all areas or most areas under their stated authority. This is highly irrational and completely unreasonable to expect of anyone, but I have witnessed this naïve assumption more than once in my years of organizational leadership from a second chair perspective. To be fair, there are rare first chair leaders who seem to foster this kind of unrealistic ideation. They seem to want everyone to think they are that good! Only God is omniscient and, as the priest in the movie, *Rudy*, correctly expressed, "Two things I know, son…there is a God…and I am not Him!"[2] The best approach to this unrealistic idea is for the first chair leader to continually remind their people of their limitations and to surround themselves with competent people from an abundance of different backgrounds, experiences, and expertise. While God can do anything and knows everything, the first chair leader cannot and does not. Ironically, everyone else on the leadership team has already figured this out!

Petty Perks

If you are the first chair trumpet player in a band or jazz band, there are some definite advantages that come with the territory. First chair players usually get to play the melody. Thus, when folks leave your concert, they are often humming the tune you were playing. Also, if you are the lead trumpet in a jazz band, you get to play the higher notes. Players in the third or fourth section almost never get to play in the upper part of the range, but first chair players tend to live there. And let's face it; more people are impressed with high notes than low notes![3]

Because they typically are more virtuosic in their musical skills, first chair players typically get many more solo opportunities. Aware of this reality, composers and arrangers of band and symphonic music tend to place solos squarely in the hands of the first chair players. Finally, I have heard it said

---

2   David Anspaugh, Jerry Goldsmith, and Arthur Morton Alexander *Courage*. RUDY. USA, 1993.

3   I got to play high notes, but he got all the solos because he really was the better player. Oddly, in the jazz band, it is actually the second chair player who gets to play the solo, improvisational parts. I learned this the hard way at Georgia Governor's Honor when I was selected to play 1st chair in the jazz band while my buddy, Phil Clark, was selected 2nd chair.

that the first chair leader sometimes gets the admiration of the opposite sex before the rest of us. That could just be a rumor, but we will let them think that is the case either way.

First chair leaders in many organizations tend to live in high-profile positions. They are often the spokesperson or chief communicator for the organization. As such, they receive greater media and social media attention. Their voice and opinions tend to matter more than those sitting in lower positions in most situations. It is almost comical when a baseball team wins the World Series, or a football team wins the Super Bowl that, the person receiving the trophy is often the owner of the team rather than the head coach or most valuable players who played on the field.

> THOUGH THE PERKS MAY SEEM REAL AND EVEN UNFAIR AT TIMES, MY ATTITUDE TOWARDS THEM CAN HELP KEEP THEIR ACTUAL IMPORTANCE IN PERSPECTIVE.

Note that I called these kinds of perks petty. Though the perks may seem real and even unfair at times, my attitude towards them can help keep their actual importance in perspective. Harry Truman has been credited with saying, "It is amazing what you can accomplish if you do not care who gets the credit." John the Baptist, the forerunner of Jesus the Messiah, was keenly aware of both his role and his limitations. When his peers and followers demanded to know if he were the messiah, John was quick and decisive in his refutation of any such claims. John knew his place on the team and his role in history. When his disciples actually began to leave his entourage and follow Jesus, it was John who explained, "He must become greater, I must become less" (John 3:30). Considering the mission of the organization, the kinds of perceived perks or benefits afforded the first chair leader are inconsequential.

Influence – Inspiring to Aspire

John Maxwell is often noted for his simplistic yet comprehensive definition of leadership, stated in just three words, "Leadership is influence."[4] I think I read those words first in Oswald Sander's classic, *Spiritual Leadership*.[5]

---

4   John Maxwell, Developing the Leader Within You (Nashville: Thomas Nelson, 1993) 1.

5   J. Oswald Sanders, *Spiritual Leadership* (Chicago: Moody Publishers, 2007) 27.

Regardless of its origin, I believe it is the shortest yet most complete definition of leadership. In its rawest form, leadership does not require a formal title or position of authority. Anyone can influence another person. And that influence can be positive or negative, for their good or their detriment. Influence. That is the essence of leadership.

I was honored to attend a small group in the Philippines hosted by a retired Christian Broadcasting Network executive and highly successful businessman, Ramon Tapales. At some point in the evening, we were discussing the topic of leadership from a biblical perspective. Because I was in the country teaching leadership principles, they were asking me questions, but I found myself leaning in to learn from this amazing elder statesman and corporate leader of leaders. When my dear friend, Riki Ishak, asked Ramon to give his basic definition of leadership, Mr. Tapales slowly raised his gaze to catch our eyes and confidently asserted, "I believe leadership can be best summed up in three words: inspiring to aspire." I never forgot that moment. And I have never heard a better definition before or since.

Inspiring others to aspire to be all they have been created to become is the impetus of what it means to lead. First chair leaders have the privilege of helping others see more inside themselves than they currently recognize or acknowledge. Visionary first chair leaders help others around them see potential, capacity, and possibility for themselves and for the organizations they serve. Aspiration looks beyond the current reality to envision a future potentiality. First chair leaders influence the personal beliefs and values around them to aim higher, probe deeper, push harder, and become more than they thought possible. I cannot imagine a higher calling or more rewarding benefit. First chair leaders influence. First chair leaders inspire others to aspire.

Real Leaders Are Servants

The best first chair players are section leaders who see their role as a servant rather than a tyrant. These first chair leaders are not overly impressed with themselves but are humble and almost shocked that they get to do first chair things. This quality makes them winsome and attractive and affords them a charisma that makes people in their section proud to be a part. Further, they obviously care about the needs and desires of their teammates. Thus, they see the development of their section and everyone in their section as a personal challenge and responsibility. These exemplary first chair leaders continually weave in and out of the five leadership levels as they develop rapport, community, and developmental relationships with those in lower-level chair positions.

However, first chair players are not always prone to cultivate the talents and abilities of those to their right. After all, if you knew what they knew or could do what they do, then you might just take their place. So, the insecure first chair players tend to guard their position. As a keyboard player, I remember a time when I was afraid to let you watch me play for fear that you might steal my hot licks…Even though I had stolen everything I ever knew from other people who didn't seem to care! Rather than helping others learn the ropes, coaching them up, and helping them develop their skills, insecure leaders tend to isolate and live with a sense of scarcity rather than abundance. At the heart of their failure to develop others is typically a deep-seated insecurity that draws significance from performance rather than a deep sense of identity. For Christian believers, this security is rooted and grounded in their new identity in Jesus Christ.

The Team Is the Thing

It is not uncommon for the better players to be hidden lower in the section. These quiet, unassuming types do not typically challenge for positions. It seems they would rather make good music together for the love of the art with little or no concern for status. They are consummate professionals who show up every day and play their part with excellence and style. They don't care who gets the credit and have no desire to sit on top of the heap. They don't seem to care if you ever know their name, but they are dedicated to their art of the collective whole, creating musical magic and aesthetic wonder. Their mantra seems to be, "We get to do this," rather than, "Look what I can do!"

> THE BEST FIRST CHAIR LEADERS REALIZE THAT NONE OF US ARE AS SMART AS ALL OF US.

The best first chair leaders realize that none of us are as smart as all of us. They value the input and ideas of others on the team. These leaders invite input, ask questions, and encourage problem-solving at the lowest possible levels of the organization. There is no need for them to receive credit for their own ideas, nor would they ever dream of taking credit for the ideas generated by those sitting in lower-level chairs. When someone else is honored, they are the first to honor them publicly. When a teammate is hurting or in need, they are there to offer assistance and encouragement. And, because first chair leaders often have access to new information and strategic initiatives, the best first chair leaders are quick to share the news and paint the vision for a shared, preferred future.

Personal Reflection and Group Discussion

- Why might it be important to "feel the pain" of a first chair leader in the heart of a second chair leader? How could that help strengthen relationships? How have you felt when others took the time and energy to empathize with you in the past?

- Tracy lists some unrealistic expectations often placed on first chair leaders. How have you seen these play out in organizations you have served? What other pressures and expectations have you observed?

- Ramon's simple definition of leadership was "inspiring to aspire." Sanders wrote that "leadership is influence." How well do these brief definitions capture the essence of leadership? What would you add to make either or both more complete?

- How can you tell when a first chair leader visualizes themselves as a servant? How does this affect their attitude and the attitudes of those who follow them?

Third Chair Musings and Perspectives

Sometimes not sitting in first chair is a blessing rather than a curse. Because we don't have to defend our title, we can live more freely and generously with others around us. That was certainly my experience as I progressed into high school.

I enjoyed being the first chair trumpet through fifth, sixth, seventh, and eighth grade. However, when I entered the Winder-Barrow High School band, my band Director, Mr. E, wisely placed me in third chair behind two quite competent seniors. Charles and Vicki were their names, and they just happened to be the band captain and band co-captain that year. I soon learned that the other seniors, juniors, and sophomores sitting to my right were not appreciative—at least not initially—that I was placed above them in rank. They had never heard me play, but apparently, in our small town, there was a buzz. A bit of reputation preceded me.

I've always cared what people think about me. Probably cared too much. My best way forward that year was the path of humility and gratitude. Why not just befriend the people? I was still playing first part; I just wasn't sitting first chair. I did not realize fully at the time the wisdom and kindness Mr. Elliott had given me by not assigning me first chair. After all, I could challenge for it if I wanted to. I was pretty sure I was better than Vicki, but I think Charles could have taken me on a good day. We will never know because I never challenged them.

The apostle Paul talks about himself later in life as being able to be content with where he was and with what he had. Having lived a few trips around the sun, the wizened apostle had learned to slow himself, rejoice in the provisions he was given, and take himself a bit less seriously than he had in his formative years. As a young man, he had been driven by zeal to measure up, set things right, and live by stringent rules in hopes of perfection. But, as an older follower of Jesus, Paul learned how to be content regardless of his living conditions. His values had shifted to the point that he said, "Contentment with godliness is great gain." I was definitely working on the contentment piece!

As I look back at my freshman year experience, I can appreciate the sense of freedom I was afforded. It was kind of nice not having to play the solos. I realized I still got to play first part, so, in a sense, I had most of the perks without the pressure. And I got to enjoy my freshman year with very little pressure to prove anything. Much like the apostle Paul with his thorn in the flesh, I was constantly reminded of my lowly freshman status by the likes of "Big John," whose class ring had to be about a size 49! I became personally acquainted with his mammoth class ring as he was constantly smacking me in the back of my head to remind me that I was but a wormy freshman and not a human. A lowly freshman worm. Those were the days!

Charles had a lot of wisdom for his age. Vicki was nice and encouraging. I enjoyed becoming friends with my two senior friends. I think Charles, Vicki, and I all relaxed once we realized we weren't competing with each other. I have learned over the years that when we're not competing, we can focus on completing. In the absence of competition and striving, we are free to focus on completing both the tasks at hand and whatever needs the other person currently has. I really liked them, respected them, and think they eventually grew beyond simply tolerating me!

> I HAVE LEARNED OVER THE YEARS THAT WHEN WE'RE NOT COMPETING, WE CAN FOCUS ON COMPLETING.

Iron sharpens iron. Charles and Vicki were good trumpet players, and there was much for me to learn from them musically. Regarding trumpeting skills, Charles was much better at double-tonguing and triple tonguing than me. He had been playing three years longer and had some skills under his belt that I was just learning how to do. I could play higher, but he had mastered some techniques I had not yet developed. Just being around them made me better. And Charles was a lot better at making the "horse whinny" at the end of Sleigh Ride at the Christmas concert that Fall! Honesty compels me to confess that I never did get that right. There was always a 50-50 chance it was going to sound more like a donkey than a horse.

That year I sat in third chair.

And I learned to like it.

I really didn't mind.

I truly enjoyed being a freshman. I didn't make any unnecessary enemies by challenging two seniors just to make my ego feel better. And it gave me time to play keyboards with the rock and roll band, too. I was afforded ample opportunities to play and sing at my church as well. At the end of the year, the three of us trumpet players were featured on the classic trio, "Bugler's Holiday." Vicki insisted that I play the second part rather than the third one. By that point, it did not matter to me who played what. I was just happy to be there among my friends! What a fitting end to a great freshman year. I would always appreciate their honesty and encouragement. Their leadership in my life would help me be a better leader in my future life.

When you sit in first chair, you are responsible. You are the de facto section leader. It's your job to whip the rest of them into shape and motivate them to practice, learn their parts, march their steps, and work together as a team. The buck stops with you. You have the authority to call a section rehearsal. The Director looks to you to police and coach all the players downline from you. Their performance reflects on you and provides commentary on your leadership.

But, when you sit in third chair, you are not responsible—at least not directly. You get to play first part, but you don't have to be in charge. In many ways, it is much easier to enjoy the journey. The buck doesn't stop with you. But that doesn't mean people do not take their cues from watching you as it relates to the way you support the first chair. I understood next year I would be sitting in the driver's seat of the section, so my approach was much akin to the golden rule of doing unto others as I would have them do unto me in the future. Pay it forward. I liked Charles and Vicki, so it was quite easy for me to support them. It wasn't long before I found myself encouraging him and protecting him when others would offer throwaway comments of criticism. And Charles would deputize Vicki and me to work with the second and third trumpets to make sure they knew their parts, played the correct notes, and kept in step on the field. When you have great teamwork and a worthy goal, it honestly does not matter where you sit in the organization.

> WHEN YOU HAVE GREAT TEAMWORK AND A WORTHY GOAL, IT HONESTLY DOES NOT MATTER WHERE YOU SIT IN THE ORGANIZATION.

We took a lot of pride in our trumpet section. And I found it easier to relate to other players seated lower in the section when I wasn't the section leader. There was less distance between my mind and their mind. I was one of them. I could feel their pain. I could see things from their perspective.

People watched how I carried myself as a freshman sitting alongside two seniors in the first trumpet section. Was I loyal to our leader? Did I talk behind his back? Would I follow his lead? Did I support him to his face and to his back? I think I did, and I believe Charles would say the same. I enjoyed my time with them, and I missed them when they were gone. I also believe that the way I followed as a freshman helped me lead as a sophomore. Good followers make good leaders. But great followers make great leaders. Clay Scroggins sums it up quite well, "Practice leading through influence when you're not in charge. It's the key to leading well when you are."[6]

Personal Reflection and Group Discussion

- Tracy claims, "When we're not competing, we can focus on completing." In what ways can competition be both a good thing and a bad thing for teams or organizations? What might it mean to 'complete' someone?

- Have you experienced seasons in your life where you had to wait to enjoy promotion or recognition? What lessons did you learn from those times? Was it easy or difficult for you?

6   Clay Scroggins, *How to Lead When You're Not in Charge* (Grand Rapids: Zondervan, 2017) 33.

- What kinds of benefits might you enjoy if you are not ultimately responsible? Are there tangible benefits you can focus on and enjoy? Are there opportunities you might not have otherwise?

- Scroggins says, "Practice leading through influence when you're not in charge. It's the key to leading well when you are." What are some of the observations you have made while not being in charge that you would want to include in your leadership should you be given that opportunity? What are some things you might want to avoid or change?

Second Chair Mindsets and Attitudes

As I learned in my time playing from third chair, in healthy, life-giving organizations, it doesn't really matter what chair you sit in or where you find yourself on the seating chart. Good things are in store, and growth is likely, expected, and cultivated as part of the fabric of the organizational culture. If you find yourself in a healthy organizational culture, you should count yourself blessed.

However, every organization is not experiencing health and may not be life-giving at all. Many second chair leaders fight to maintain a positive attitude as they face significant challenges navigating political agendas, unclear expectations, communication gaps, and low levels of trust among team members. While many of us are enjoying the blessing of thriving, others are fighting to survive. Part of the frustration in leading from second chair is the realization that we cannot control many of the issues that contribute to organizational health or dysfunction. What we can control, however, is our mindset and our attitude.

The Perspective Collective

I shared earlier that Dr. Don Hight coined the phrase, "Where you sit is where you stand." Your perspective influences your outlook. Where you sit in the organization allows you a unique perspective. You may see things others don't even notice or may not even know exist. Or you may miss things that others consider plainly in view and obvious. Second chair leaders have direct access to perspectives from almost every angle in the organization because of the strategic access they have to people: people above, around, and under them. We are closer to the front lines; thus, we can see, hear, and experience their perspectives. We have colleagues and teammates around us who provide their perspectives. And we have some level of access to the people in first chair. We have access to the perspective collective if we will leverage our access by listening closely, continuously, and actively.

Any bus driver worth their salt knows there are things going on in the back of the bus that they simply can't see or hear from their seat in the front of the bus. Therefore, the driver needs an extra set of eyes and ears to gain perspective on what's happening inside the bus. The driver needs you to sit where you sit so they can see what you see, hear what you hear, and feel what you feel. Similarly, those colleagues and coworkers assembled around your seat need you to speak up and stand up as an advocate on their behalf from time to time. They need you to stand where you sit. Helping people 'stand where they sit' implies helping others grow, learn, improve, and add value to each other at all points and at all times. But this only works if your organization is a listening and learning organization where opinions are valued, voices are not silenced, and honest dialogue is welcomed without fear of penalty.

IT IS POSSIBLE TO BE BLINDED BY VISION WHILE DEAF TO THE CURRENT SITUATION.

If the only voices allowed to be heard are those of senior leadership or first chair leaders, the organization will miss valuable insights and perspectives. Not only will they likely miss important grassroots information, but they may also become tone-deaf to the nuances of attitudes and feelings among the rank and file. It is possible to be blinded by vision while deaf to the current situation.

My mom reminded me occasionally that some people are "so heavenly-minded they're of no earthly good!" I have worked in organizations that historically listened to the voices of each constituency and provided forums for civil discourse in some situations but abandoned those practices for a season as pressures increased, deadlines pressed in, and only the voices of senior leadership addressed the problems at hand. The season that followed was a painful reminder that echo chambers tend to produce shortsighted decisions. The people felt like they were not heard, and their concerns or ideas were not considered. There was a total lack of buy-in or support. People were hurt, emotions ran high, and morale plummeted. In retrospect, it was clear that many of these consequences may have been averted if second chair leaders had been consulted and allowed to advocate. We seemed to have forgotten that none of us was as smart as all of us. **As inconvenient and time-consuming as the process of listening may be for our leadership teams, too much hangs in the balance when we ignore or disregard the collective perspective within our people.**

But if the organization values the insights, perspectives, and feelings of everyone regardless of their seat on the bus, the voices of those in the back or in obscure locations will matter and be heard. Wise leaders understand that the best solutions typically are generated closest to the problem. Proximity to the issue can lead to insight and nuanced understanding that would otherwise be missed by those outside the range of sight and sound.

Grassroots problems require grassroots solutions. Empowerment begins when first chair leaders listen and trust the perspectives and problem-solving capacity of those in the lower seats. That's why we need to solve problems at the lowest possible level. The perspective collective is one of the superpowers of exemplary second chair leadership.

Right People, Right Seats

Jim Collins taught us that getting the right people on the bus is the first challenge of leadership.[7] According to Collins, the second challenge is getting the right people in the right seats on the bus. It is quite possible to secure the right people on the team while placing them in the wrong position. Placing people according to their personal bent, present capacity, and to the best advantage of the team is a never-ending responsibility of leadership. It takes time, attention, and intention to see the golden treasure hidden in each person on the team and direct them to the place they can make the most significant contribution. Admittedly, we may need to intentionally ask people to serve our organization in an area that is less suited for them for a temporary season of time while we orchestrate a plan to move them into their sweet spot in the future when the timing is right. But Dupree is correct: getting the right people on the bus is half the equation, while getting them in the right seats is the other half. Right people, right seats.

I was privileged to play with four outstanding musicians in the Athens Brass Quintet during my freshman year at UGA. I sat second chair to Phil Clarke.

7   Jim Collins, *Good to Great* (New York: HarperCollins, 2001).

Phil was my friend and the best trumpet player at the college at the time. I loved his compact sound and silky dark tone. His technique, style, and finesse inspired me to work harder, imitate what I heard, and grow into the position of second chair to complement the virtuosity Phil consistently displayed. My goal was to become a sponge and soak up all I could while playing across from him. I honestly believe my best playing happened in that quintet during my freshman year. My sound became more compact, and my tone sweetened! In a brass quintet, the first chair trumpet player is the one you rely upon for setting the tempo, starting the song, cut-offs, and indication of any tempo changes during the musical interchange. Phil was the right man for the job. His leadership transformed my followership. His influence made me better, and our quintet made some beautiful music together in spite of me.

My wife, Lisa, continually reminded our children, Justin and Jordan, that there are always people smarter than you, faster than you, more talented than you, better looking than you and that our best approach is to become the best version of ourselves we can possibly be. Get better. Improve. Shoot for your personal best. Be honest with yourself about your limitations and status but keep growing.

ONE OF THE HALLMARKS OF EMOTIONAL SECURITY AND MATURITY IS THE ABILITY TO CELEBRATE THE TALENTS AND SUCCESS OF OTHERS.

Once we have accepted our position and bought into it, we are no longer competing with anyone but ourselves. One of the hallmarks of emotional security and maturity is the ability to celebrate the talents and success of others who may be better than us or more naturally gifted than we are. We can learn to lean into their competence, learn from their experience, and temper our expectations along the way.

Our daughter, Jordan, had a flair for alto saxophone. If you knew Jordan, you would know that she is always going to be humble, kind, and respectful of others. She cares what others think, and she honestly cares about them as people. She was satisfied to sit in second chair though she played better technically and had a nicer sound than the guy sitting to her left. And Jordan hated solos. She never wanted to be in the limelight. It gave her an upset stomach! So, Jordan decided to make the most of second chair. She got to play first alto sax parts without the pressure of soloing. It was a win/win situation. Jordan enjoyed the honor of playing in an amazing high school band program from the vantage point of second chair. Though her Dad always thought she should have been the first chair, I believe she sat in the right seat on the bus for her.

Attitude Determines Altitude

Your attitude will determine your altitude. Nothing ruins organizational morale and culture like a bad attitude. I call it stinking thinking. Bad attitudes can be cancerous malignancies on our team. And stinking thinking is highly contagious. My mindset or mental outlook will determine or deter my professional career. My attitude determines my emotional climate. Am I positive or negative in my outlook, perceptions, emotions, and persona? Do I see the glass half empty or half full? Do I

> GOOD, BAD, OR UGLY, I WILL RISE OR FALL TO THE LEVEL OF MY ATTITUDE.

tend to be optimistic about the future or pessimistic? Do I see problems or potentialities? Do I envision obstacles or opportunities? Good, bad, or ugly, I will rise or fall to the level of my attitude.

We choose our attitudes. It is common to talk about getting up on the wrong side of the bed or waking up with a bad attitude. By lunchtime on any given day, we've decided whether today is a good day or a bad day. We might even say things to each other like, "I'm having a really bad day." In such cases, we have allowed our feelings, emotions, physical challenges, or circumstances to negatively influence our mental mindset and emotional outlook. They become the lenses through which we see our day. As a result, my outlook sours. My productivity stalls. Rather than acting with confidence and stability, I hesitate or make choices erratically.

To be clear, bad things happen, and everything does not always come easy. Life is unpleasant, people are rude, traffic is crazy, nothing goes the way I think it should, and my expectations can get sidetracked in a split second. But, at every point along the way, we have made choices regarding our response or reaction to the current conditions in and around us. I made the choices, but I could have made better ones. My attitude has affected my altitude. And, by mid-day, I have made the premature determination that the day falls into the category of 'bad day.' My altitude is sinking as my attitude sours. My attitude affects me personally. But, have I ever considered how my attitude affects the altitude of those around me as well?

> **HONEST FEEDBACK FROM PEOPLE WHO CARE ABOUT US IS AMONG THE GREATEST POTENTIAL GIFTS WE CAN EVER RECEIVE.**

One sure way to know is to ask the people around you the question, "What is it like to be on the other side of me?" Honest feedback from people who care about us is among the greatest potential gifts we can ever receive. We may be shocked to learn that the way we perceive ourselves and our attitudes may be very different from the actual experience others have in our presence. It may be hard to hear their response, and the question probably scares the liver out of you but take a deep breath and ask the question. What is it like to be on the other side of me? Then, listen carefully to what they say and how they frame it. Don't push back. Lean in. Fight the urge to defend and talk back. Even if what they say is distorted and biased, look for the kernel of truth and learn.

You can gain insight by paying attention to the responses of others as you speak. In many instances, I find that my content may be spot on, but my delivery is lacking. There may not be an issue concerning what I am saying, but my tone or volume level, or choice of words may color my message and reveal a deeper issue of attitude. While we may pick up on the throw-away negative or cynical comments of others, we may completely miss or dismiss those same kinds of words from our own conversations. I am typically a very encouraging and positive person, but there are times when someone pushes my buttons, and I am less than kind, abrupt, and forceful. This is particularly true when I'm stressed or under pressure. My attitude or emotional climate colors my tone and changes the message I am sending as it is perceived by the receiver. We need relational mirrors to help us see the flaws within our attitudes and help us navigate a route to improvement. It is easier than we realize to drift into patterns of stinking thinking while believing we are maintaining a positive outlook and demeanor. Ask. Listen. Learn. Grow.

Regardless of where I sit in the organization, how I think and respond affects my performance. And it often affects the performance and outlook of those near me as well. People do what people see. I can become either an emotional asset or emotional liability to my teammates by my choice of attitude. My altitude is affected, but if I am honest with myself, the people around me are also negatively influenced by my attitude as well. Attitude matters to me and those around me. Recognize it and take responsibility for cultivating a better attitude for your sake and theirs. Watch the body language of your peers when you speak. Pay attention to the distance they are keeping from you. Learn to recognize that nasty smell as the aroma of your own stinking thinking and determine to change both your attitude and altitude.

Mike Bonem & Roger Patterson (page 22) list four attitudes as essential to thriving in service to any organization: an attitude of submission, an attitude of service, an attitude of being thankful, and an attitude of passion.[8] Humility, helpfulness, gratitude, and enthusiasm are winsome and contagious. Choose your attitude well. Catch yourself being good in your attitude. Celebrate that and strive to repeat that mindset. Catch yourself being bad in your attitude. Admit it and determine to change the direction of your affection in the middle of your bad day. Transforming your attitude has the potential to transform, at some level or to some degree, the attitude of all those within the sphere of your influence. I have noticed in life that bad attitudes seldom get rewarded. If you don't like where you sit, you might be well advised to take notice of your attitude as you sit there. And if you notice others sitting farther and farther away from you, it could be a cue to bathe better or give yourself a serious attitude check. Attitude determines altitude. Mine and theirs.

Work Hard, Work Smart

Show respect for everyone, especially those beside you and beneath you. Learning their name is the first and last sign of true respect. People love to hear their names, so learn them and use them regularly. I really must work hard at this. One of my former pastors had a method for memorizing names by learning the family tree as a kind of filing system he used for name retrieval. It seems counterintuitive, but it worked for him. It was quite impressive that he knew my name, my wife's name, my kids' names, and any relevant relationships to our network. I do well to remember you and your family!

8   Mike Bonem and Roger Patterson, *Leading from the Second Chair* (Minneapolis: Fortress Press, 2020) 22-23.

DO EVERYTHING THEY ASK YOU TO DO, AND THEN SOME.

Do everything they ask you to do, and then some. Arrive early, and stay late if necessary. Don't watch the clock or bolt out the exit door the minute the day is over. Come prepared for meetings. Do your due diligence. Don't stop short; follow through. Arrive at meetings no less than five minutes early and help with logistics. Engage with others from start to finish. Answer questions succinctly and clearly. If you don't know, ask someone. Keep your phone on silent and turn it facedown on the table or leave it in your office during meetings. Take notes, particularly regarding the next steps or any form of deliverable that will be expected of you or your team. Write yourself reminders of anything you need to discuss or questions that come to mind during the meeting but are inappropriate to ask in the moment. Don't rush out the door at the end. Help clean up when it's over. Call your colleagues by name.

Pace yourself. Whatever you do in the first couple of weeks, they will expect from you moving forward. Set good boundaries. Honor your day off and those of your co-workers. Let nothing be beneath you. Never ask others to do anything you're not willing to do yourself. Remember, people would rather see a sermon than hear one most any day. Be a thermostat. Set the emotional climate with positivity, cheerfulness, compassion, kindness, and winsome behavior. Take initiative. Solve problems. Assume that the need is your call to engage and your opportunity to serve. Be a go-to person. I like to think of myself as a utility infielder, ready at any moment for the coach to place me in at any point. Be an impact person. Make a difference. Make yourself valuable. Strive for excellence in every area.

Competing or Completing?

I am either here to compete with you or help complete you. Compete or complete. One letter makes all the difference. No, I don't think there's anything wrong with healthy competition if everyone is better in the end. If we all buy into and embrace the same mission as a team or organization, then our goal is to see the organization complete the mission regardless of the cost, the time it takes to achieve the mission or the role we play on the team. But to reach that level of buy-in, the focus for second chair leaders must shift from *me* to *others* and from *competing* to *completing*.

At Clarke Central high school football camp, every evening, the offense would line up against the defense and walk through what they called "perfect plays." This provided a visualization of what could happen if everyone played their part and successfully accomplished their role during the play. If the play was run perfectly, no matter what play they were running now, the offense could score. Obviously, this kind of thinking completely discounts the presence of a competent defense! It assumes that every offensive player at each position whips his opponent on defense. That's what makes it perfect, I suppose. I think an even more important lesson learned when it comes to perfect plays is that my role in every play makes a huge difference in the potential success or failure of any play called by the offensive coordinator. If I don't do my job or play my part successfully, the play won't work, and the team will not be successful at that moment in time. My imperfection will ruin the perfect play.

If I can understand and buy into that mindset and perspective, I will be much less likely to compete with the person on my left or my right. I will care far more deeply about their success and will do all I can to help them succeed, as well as give everything within me to do a great job myself. In a world where perfect plays potentially win ballgames and help us achieve our goals as a team, every role and position matters. There are no unimportant roles. In essence, it doesn't matter where you sit when you play if you buy into the mission of the team.

One example I regularly observe as a true Southerner and lover of college football is the challenge between two gifted athletes competing for the same job as a starting quarterback on an elite football team. How ironic is it that while one of those elite athletes is on the field performing, the one on the sidelines has an opportunity to either compete or complete the goals of the team by the way the sidelined athlete helps the starter succeed? Their success determines the success of the team; however, their individual success off the field may be the prime indicator of whether they get a chance to perform on the field or not. What an enigma! In a best-case scenario, the quarterback on the sideline must support the quarterback on the field while remaining ever-ready and prepared to enter the game at a moment's notice should the starter be unable to play. The same would be true about any position on the team but is more readily apparent and obvious at the quarterback position.

We've heard the old adages: "A rising tide lifts all the boats in the harbor, not just mine." and "The needs of the many outweigh the needs of the few (or the one)." It's easy enough to read such statements. But to truly live as though the mission of the team trumps my personal ambition is far from easy and even farther from natural. A great deal of maturity is required in all of us as we strive to complete the team by serving faithfully in the roles we are assigned, whether or not we are on the field or hidden somewhere on the sidelines. Perhaps this is yet another reason why so very few teams are considered elite. Competition can blind us and bind us from completing the mission and contributing to the completion of the other players on the team.

In his book *A New Kind of Diversity*, Tim Elmore offers a strategy called "reverse mentoring" as a means of helping intergenerational teams overcome the challenges of generation gaps in the workplace.[9] This strategy is also a fantastic example of what competing yielding to completing can look like on the ground. Reverse mentoring is almost the opposite of traditional mentoring, where the older person takes the younger protégé under their wing to train or develop them. In reverse mentoring, the younger person takes on the role of trainer, and the older person becomes the protégé. The assumption behind the practice is that we can learn from everyone, anywhere and anytime. By humbly asking for assistance from the younger generations around us on our teams, we can model the completing mindset and alleviate the need for competition as a result.

Personal Reflection and Group Discussion

- How is sitting in second chair conducive to gathering a variety of perspectives? Why is it important to understand and value the perspectives of others?

- Tracy says, "It is possible to be blinded by vision while deaf to the current situation." What does that mean, and how could it prove harmful to the organization? What strategies do you suggest for gaining proper perspective while staying on mission?

---

9   Tim Elmore, *A New Kind of Diversity* (Atlanta: Maxwell Leadership, 2022).

- Have you ever experienced a time where you were on the right bus but serving in the wrong seat? What advice would you give someone who finds themselves in that situation currently?

- How does our attitude affect the climate of our team or organization? Have you taken the opportunity to ask your closest associates what it is like to be on the other side of you? Where do you need the most work around attitude adjustments?

- What do you think about the idea of reverse mentoring? Can you think of examples where the older generation can learn from the younger? What next steps can you take to begin this practice in your life or organization?

Second Chair Limitations

Every position not only has its vantage points and advantage points but also its limitations. While there are areas we are responsible for managing and tasks we are held accountable to perform, there are limits to our responsibilities, our scope of influence, our rights, and our privileges. Second chair leaders, like all leaders, have limitations. It is vital to know our limitations, but it is equally important to live within the boundaries as well. This chapter explores the parameters and perimeters of second chair leadership.

Follow the Leader

As second chair leaders in performing ensembles, we ultimately follow the lead of the director or conductor. The director is recognized as the chief leader of the organization. All the first chair leaders lead the way in following the directions of the director. Similarly, we follow the leadership of our section, the person sitting in first chair. However, once the curtain is pulled and the downbeat is given, the ensemble yields its trust and attention to the sole leadership of the person with the baton. We follow the ultimate leader, the director. Having been the dean of a department and vice president of a division of a Christian liberal arts college for fifteen years, I can recall many times when I was clearly the person in charge of the meeting; however, whenever the president walked in, my authority was overruled, and I relinquished the baton to my organizational senior leader.

In healthy organizations, the first chair or departmental leaders orchestrate and facilitate the mission, vision, values, and strategic initiatives of the respective division while ultimately following and aligning the department with the ultimate mission, vision, values, and strategic initiatives of the organization. As a youth pastor, I led teams of adult and student leaders as we achieved together the collective mission, vision, values, and strategic initiatives exclusive to our department. All the while, we were in constant communication and interaction with the global mission, vision, values, and strategic initiatives of the church and the Senior Pastor. The same process held true for every other department of the church.

Every second chair leader operates within a framework of delegated responsibility, accountability, alignment, and assessment to preclude any sense of mission drift or misalignment. There are definite limits, limitations, and boundaries to be honored. Clear job descriptions help define the roles and reporting relationships within a particular job assignment. In certain situations, you may have the role of final authority, while in other circumstances, you may have referential authority while reserving the final approval for your direct report upstream. Following the leader requires taking the initiative when it is mine to take while yielding to the first chair at other times and situations.

Not My Job

I am reminded of the character Chico, from the 1970s hit television sitcom *Chico and the Man*. Freddy Prinze, who played the character Chico Rodriguez on the show. Chico made famous the line, "It's not my job, man!"[10] While Chico typically used that line to avoid doing whatever needed to be done at the moment, it is a reminder to each of us that our roles have boundaries and territories with limits to be honored and roles to be clearly defined to avoid confusion or ambiguity. The first limitation we must learn is that sitting in first chair is not our job. Being the boss is not our job. We are not the top dog. We do not occupy the corner office. We do not sit atop the organizational hierarchy or flow chart. It's not our job.

> THE FIRST LIMITATION WE MUST LEARN IS THAT SITTING IN FIRST CHAIR IS NOT OUR JOB.

A few months ago, I was asked to serve as the Campus Pastor for a satellite church about thirty minutes away from the campus of our home church. I

10   Chico and the Man. 1974. Season 1, Episode 1. "Pilot." Directed by Komack, James. Aired on September 13, 1974 on NBC.

had been meeting with them on most Sundays and Wednesdays for a couple of months and was enjoying the budding relationships and mounting momentum. To formalize the role, my senior pastor agreed to come down and meet with the congregation the following Sunday at a luncheon on the satellite church campus. When my pastor and his wife arrived, I was amazed at the sense of love and respect they were instantly given by the congregation of our little church. I was instantly reminded that I was not the first chair leader. My pastor is the senior pastor, and I am the campus pastor. While I am in charge in most circumstances and provide frontline pastoral care and leadership, I serve at the pleasure and discretion of my lead pastor. While my role as campus pastor often resembles a first chair leadership role, it is a second chair position at the end of the day. I am not the senior pastor. It is not my job.

That declaration is not necessarily a limitation, but it is a clarification. Clear job descriptions are critical for effective and efficient organizations. **Knowing what not to do can be as clarifying as knowing what to do.** Countless times in my career, a

KNOWING WHAT NOT TO DO CAN BE AS CLARIFYING AS KNOWING WHAT TO DO.

reminder that "it is not my job" brought a sigh of relief. I'm glad it's not my job more days than not. But, if I'm completely honest, that's not true every day or in every way. People who sit in second chair don't get to set the vision or chart the ultimate course. In healthy organizations, they may get to speak to it, have a voice in it, or sit at the table around those who do. But, at the end of the day, it's not my job.

What Is My Job?

As second chair musicians, it is our job to play our part, know our music well, practice our parts between rehearsals, correct any mistakes, and prepare in advance. Practice precedes rehearsal. Practice is done single file on an individual basis, but rehearsal is an interaction between those of us who have been trusted to practice in preparation for the group rehearsal. In organizational leadership, we must know our role before we can play our part. It is not enough to simply know what we are not responsible for, but we must know and embrace our roles and responsibilities. We must know what our job is and all that it entails if we are going to be successful. Considering that reality, what are some of the jobs that commonly fall into the general realm of responsibility for most second chair leaders?

Competence is our first job. Every second chair leader is expected to be skilled and capable of doing their job and doing it well. Similarly, it is our job to know our stuff and find answers to any questions before assembling as a team. In the musical context, it may mean listening to recordings of the song played by exemplary ensembles. It may mean asking other players in our section and around us for help with parts. It may even mean organizing small clusters of rehearsals before rehearsing as a section. But, at the very least, it means practicing my part so that I can play it in context and at the right tempo with increasing clarity and excellence. Second chair leaders are expected to know their part and play it with excellence. That is job one.

In an instrumental ensemble or section of that ensemble, it is also my job to balance my part with all the other parts in the section. I need to play clearly, distinctly, and loud enough to be heard yet soft enough to never obscure the clarity and perception of all the other parts. Not too soft, not too loud, but just right. It's my job to blend with all the other instruments in my section. This has to do with tone quality or the unique sound and beauty of the sound of my horn. Brass players tend to play too brightly, causing their part to stand out and draw attention to itself. It may sound harsh or tinny or thin. Occasionally, someone may play too darkly or in a muted way, causing their sound to be subdued and lost in the mix among the other players in the section. Once again, it needs to be not too bright, not too dark, but just right. Balanced and blended.

One issue that can cause us to be out of balance and unblended more quickly than almost any other attribute of playing in a section is the issue of intonation or playing in tune. This has to do with the highness or lowness of a particular pitch in relation to all the other players in your section. To be sure, there is a standard pitch to which we all must tune our instruments before we begin to play. In most orchestras around the world, the standard pitch is A440. In most bands, which are typically orchestras minus the string players, we tune to concert B-flat. However, just because we can tune that one note does not ensure that every other note will be played in tune consistently. While many people may not know if something is played perfectly in tune, they probably do know when something is played grossly out of tune. They may not know what to call it, but they know it is unpleasant to the ears. To successfully play for the benefit of a section, every player needs to play every note in tune with themselves and the person sitting to the left and the right.

Then there are issues with the style of playing as well as keeping time, holding notes the proper duration, and interpreting the music uniformly within the section at the direction of the Director ultimately, but occasionally through the interpretation of the section leader or the person sitting in first chair. Who knew music could be so complicated, huh?

As in instrumental ensembles, organizations require second chair leaders to be competent and skilled. You are expected to perform your specific roles and responsibilities effectively and efficiently. You are also expected to manage your teams well. Knowing the strengths and weaknesses of your teammates will help in placing them in positions where they can also thrive and be energized as well. It is my role to make sure their voices are heard, understood, and represented well when their input is required. Achieving clear communication is imperative. Handling conflicting voices, hearing concerns, and working to achieve sustained team unity is a role of second chair leaders as well. Motivating team members to know their roles, prepare effectively, and execute well are my roles additionally. Keeping my team in step with the overall direction of the organization is one of my chief concerns as a second chair leader. These are all part of my job.

When I agreed to serve as Vice President for Student Development at Emmanuel College, I had no idea what that would entail. During my earlier years at the college, I had previously served as Campus Pastor on the Student Life team, so I was aware that campus spiritual life, worship services, small groups, service teams, global missions initiatives, and such fell within the departmental oversight domain. But, who knew that student housing administration, residential programming, staff residence directors, student residence assistants, student conduct, Title IX oversight, intramural sports, student government, student organizations, clubs, counseling, crisis counseling, emotional support animals, campus security, career services, campus life programming, leadership training initiatives, student grievances, budgeting, financial administration, new student orientation, student handbooks, early alert intervention systems, health services, campus safety annual reports, and the campus phone app all fell under the massive umbrella of student development? Certainly not me.

The former Vice President of Student Development, Jason, had been a student of mine during my campus pastor years. He was a brilliant leader and had assembled an amazing team of qualified, competent men and women to handle all these functions and oversee each area. My learning curve was steep, but I knew the team could educate me and bring me up to speed if I could learn to empower them, take risks, and stay out of their way while simultaneously supporting them. Further, I had the privilege of retaining Jason on my team as he worked on his next degree in counseling and made himself available to help me limp through my new responsibilities. Our greatest resource was and is the people on our team.

Did I mention that I hate meetings?

Well, that is not completely true.

I hate meandering, meaningless meetings—I have attended and led my fair share of those!

Education, and particularly higher education, is built around meetings. Many, many meetings. But, despite my disdain for seemingly endless or needless meetings, I felt the need to meet with my team more regularly. In fact, I expanded our team to include liaisons from strategic areas in our weekly meetings. We had to bring in chairs from outside the room and crammed more people in that room than the fire marshal would have appreciated. Most of these leaders had rarely, if ever, been included in the decision-making processes in their areas or, at least, in the larger concerns of the department. And we barely knew each other. What had once been a tightly knit family had drifted into a finely tuned organization that ran their departments well but hardly interacted with the other people on the larger team. I strongly believed that needed to change. But that meant more meetings.

Smaller Christian liberal arts colleges tend to struggle financially. Securing endowments and fundraising are the critical transactions separating financially flourishing institutions from those that tend to rely on tuition fees for survival. I had begun to appreciate this truth as a dean of a department, but it became even more apparent as a vice president. Much of our weekly senior leadership meetings centered around financial planning, budgeting, and initiatives to increase revenue while continuing both the academic excellence and student engagement required for success in higher education.

One Wednesday afternoon, our senior leadership meeting was more intense and gut-wrenching as we faced the extreme challenge of balancing a budget that was headed toward disaster if we could not quickly identify and eliminate some large expenditures. But it also meant agreement to significantly cut the budgets we had painstakingly created just weeks before. We were given forty-eight hours to compile our departmental budget reduction proposals to reach the overall percentage cuts needed to potentially correct our spending overages.

Some of my vice president colleagues did not have teams to assist them with these decisions. Others felt it was their responsibility to make those decisions and assume the role of the bad guy. I was somewhat conflicted as I have always believed that problems should be handled at the lowest possible levels and that input from others was vital for ownership of solutions. However, I also felt responsible and that the buck should stop with me. I should make the tough

I WAS TEMPTED TO IGNORE MY IDEALS AND TAKE A TOP-DOWN APPROACH.

calls and own them. I was tempted to ignore my ideals and take a top-down approach. Ignoring the simpler, less time-consuming route was tempting, but I could not help sensing that too much hung in the balance if I did not include my team and get their input and ownership. I would let them voluntarily choose what they would cut and how much they would cut their precious funds for student activities. Time was not on my side. So, I called an emergency meeting with the directors for late that afternoon.

The next decision was how much information I should give them. Should I tell them the full scope of the problem, prescribe a required reduction percentage, or simply provide an overview and see where it landed? At that moment, I decided that less information was the best way forward and gave my team leaders until noon the next day to send me their proposed budget cuts. If I am completely honest, I was unsure they would cut deeply enough. After all, I had trained them to be the strongest advocates for their budgets and proposals. But I knew they would think, pray, and respond as they felt appropriate.

Early the next afternoon, I was shocked as I read the proposed budget cuts from these amazing team leaders. All of them had made significant sacrifices. It was painful for all of us. It hurt my heart to ask them to make these tough decisions, but I marveled at their commitment to the college and its continued sustained success. Their combined efforts, plus my own deep cuts, allowed us to reach our assigned figures without a second round of cuts or negotiations. I am ashamed to admit that I almost did not give them the opportunity to make these decisions themselves, but I have never been more proud of any team I have ever had the privilege to serve. That experience taught me to trust my teams and team leaders more than ever.

Clear Expectations

Establish clear expectations before you begin. If there is no job description, humbly create one and submit it to your superior for discussion, editing, and clear understanding before you work one day. Gain clarity around practical issues like office hours, dress code, days off, vacations, sick leave, tax withholdings, medical insurance, retirement benefits, personal leave days, staff development provisions, worker's compensation, life insurance, working from home, maternity/paternity leave, work computers and software, staff meetings, purchase orders, reimbursable expenses, housing allowances, moving expenses, email, websites, communication systems, social media, keys, alarm codes, voicemail, and anything else you need clear communication around. I encourage you to prepare a checklist and get as much information before your first day as possible. You'll thank me for this one.

> I CONSTANTLY REMINDED MYSELF THAT THE ONLY DUMB QUESTION WAS THE ONE I FAILED TO ASK.

If they provide you with a policy manual, read it. Highlight areas that may seem unclear and ask the proper person for explanations to achieve clarity. Do not be afraid to ask questions. Ask other staff members in similar positions your workplace questions. If you are new to the organization, you may want to ask people to give you their names multiple times over the first few weeks. I constantly reminded myself that the only dumb question was the one I failed to ask. Seek clarity around the expectations the organization and your leaders have of you. If expectations are unclear and nonspecific, there are bound to be disappointments that may have easily been avoidable with a bit of digging for answers for the sake of mutual clarity.

Additional Expectations

Other Duties as Assigned. Every job I have ever held has included additional duties and expectations beyond the stated job description. In most cases, there is no job description for any of these responsibilities. They are assumed. Implied. Expected, though not actually stated. As with any field of expertise or endeavor, there are baseline expectations inherent to the position that are virtually assumed and expected to be withheld without the need to spell them out explicitly. Preachers are assumed to have baseline communication skills. Pastors are assumed to have certain people skills. Chefs are expected to have mastered certain basic culinary skills. And, accordingly, if you do not fulfill these expectations consistently and skillfully, you could lose your seat to someone else in your section and find yourself even further down line than second chair. Or you could be asked to leave.

It Depends on the Scope. Then there is the issue of scope. In bands and orchestras, some sections are quite large with multiple individuals playing the same part, while other sections may only have one person per part. While the composer may have scored three different trumpet parts, there may be 15 trumpet players playing those three parts or 25 clarinets playing their three different parts. Yet, in an orchestra, there may be three or four trumpet parts and only three or four trumpet players. The level of responsibility placed on an orchestral second chair trumpet player could prove to be critical as you may be the only person responsible for playing your assigned part. The reasoning for this is that brass instruments are acoustically much louder than string instruments, thus creating a need for proportionately more string players than brass players to balance things acoustically across the orchestra. Thus, there are limitations on the actual availability of positions depending on the instrument you play. Orchestras need many more string players than brass or percussionists.

Depending on the size and nature of the organization, there may be a limited number of available second chair positions. A small church paid staff would be quite small in comparison to a church with several thousand members. Third and fourth chair positions are often much more plentiful. The same small church may utilize dozens of volunteers with only one paid associate staff pastor on board, or the megachurch may have hundreds of third and fourth chair positions with a few dozen second chair associates. A fast-food restaurant chain may hire two or three shift managers, with dozens of crew members required for each shift. The scope of the organization would have an impact on the kinds of requirements for the second chair position and the visibility of the actual second chair role. In my department at the college, I served in a second chair role as a vice president but had a dozen direct report employees, support employees, and large numbers of student leaders under our departmental direction.

First Chair in Waiting. One other piece of interesting information is that the second chair player becomes the first chair player in the absence of the first chair player. Therefore, it is advisable that the second chair player know both his part and that of the first chair player. Like the vice president of the United States, you may have only a perfunctory leadership role as the vice president until the president can no longer carry out their duties. Suddenly you are the president, and you are the first chair leader. No pressure! I never said it was easy. Similarly, if you are an associate pastor, you always need to have a sermon in your back pocket just in case the lead pastor is ill or is unable to fill their role as preaching pastor on any given Sunday. One of my former students was suddenly thrust into the role of senior pastor when his beloved pastor suffered a massive heart attack and passed away on the day before Easter Sunday. While we may have little to no control over the circumstances, it would be wise for second chair leaders to be prepared for these types of contingencies.

Find Your Lane

Discover your boundaries. Find your lane and stay in it. Some organizations can be territorial. Your colleagues have probably fought long and hard to attain the assets, facilities, equipment, and supplies they currently have. Get permission before using them so you will not have to ask for forgiveness later. Rome was not built in a day. Better to work slowly, methodically, and steadily than to rush

> CELEBRATE WHAT YOU HAVE AND BE GRATEFUL FOR IT. REFUSE TO BE TERRITORIAL.

in and set world records for completion rates and speed of service rendered. Celebrate what you have and be grateful for it. Refuse to be territorial. Share what you have and offer your assistance as you have time. Remember that people are your most appreciable assets.

Additional Limitations

One often overlooked limitation is limited perspective. You can only see, hear, and experience so much from where you sit in an organization. You probably don't have the same access to the Director and must lean into the first chair player for communication and updates. We have discussed earlier the need for eyes and ears from all different perspectives and vantage points, but we must also remember that our view is limited as well. Short-sightedness can result from an inability to "see the forest for the trees" or operate with the big picture in mind. As the Dean of the School of Christian Ministries, it was my job to be the chief advocate for that school, but it was critically important that I recognized there were other departments with different needs and limited funds to meet the plethora of needs throughout the college.

Another limitation is limited authority. This, of course, will depend on the culture of the organization and its expectations around the autonomy and responsibility of each player, section leader, and the various levels of trust among members at any point in time. It has been said that absolute authority corrupts absolutely. Checks and balances have been the key to our American republic for over two centuries. Marriages fall apart when the needs of both spouses are not considered and considered regularly. Exploitation, manipulation, marginalization, and inequity result when there are not appropriate checks and balances in place. As second chair leaders, we must know our limits and respect our limited authority.

Time and space do not allow for a complete discussion regarding our limits as second chair leadership. Other limiting factors could include insecurity, lack of trust, lack of communication, fear of failure, timidity, lack of confidence, lack of experience, insufficient training, lack of competence, or lack of empowerment. Recognition of our limitations is an important component if we are to succeed as second chair leaders.

In all honesty, the greatest limiting factor to leadership in any chair may be the most elusive and surprising. To catch a glimpse of this limitation, one need only look in the mirror. The most restrictive lids on my personal leadership are often self-imposed. One of the most compelling imperatives given by Jesus is the command to "love others as you love yourself" (Matthew 22:39). The implication is that it is virtually impossible to love others without first having a healthy dose of self-acceptance and appreciation of our intrinsic value. I tend to be my worst critic. I struggle to forgive myself. I often place unrealistic expectations about what I can and cannot do or what I should or should not do. With every finger I point in the direction of another person, I have four fingers pointing back at me. While the apostle Paul was clear in his encouragement not to think more highly of myself than I ought, he was equally clear that we are to regard ourselves with sober judgment.[11] It has been my personal experience that the most difficult limitations to exceed are located between my ears. Before I can become a lid-lifter for others, I may need assistance in lifting the lids I have placed on myself first. Trusted friends, counselors, parents, and mentors may be more than willing to help begin the process of removing the mirror-image lid.

Personal Reflection and Group Discussion

- "Knowing what not to do can be as clarifying as knowing what to do." Have you ever been in a situation where your job description was vague or non-existent? How did you learn what was expected or gain greater clarity? Did you ever step over a line and take on too much responsibility or come up short in meeting the expectations of your superiors?

- Competence and skill are essential to leading from any chair. Create a brief list of your top five competencies currently. Think about how you have become aware of those strengths. What was the pathway to your awareness of these competencies or strengths?

- Tracy talks about the necessity of playing in tune and finding balance within our teams. In your experience, what practices help achieve team unity? How can you discern when things or people are out of balance? How do you create and maintain balance in your personal life and teams?

- Tracy cites a time of crisis when his team was called upon to make sacrifices for the good of the organization. Can you recall times when you and your team were expected to make deep sacrifices for the good of the organization? What were the keys to handling things and people well during that time? If you had a chance to do it over, what might you change this time around?

11   Romans 12:3.

SECOND
CHAIR
6

Second Chair Vantage Points

John Maxwell describes second chair leadership as "leading from the middle of the pack."[12] If you lead from the top of the pack, you can only see so far beneath you though you can see quite far around you and ahead of you. If you lead from the bottom of the pack, you can't see very far above you or around you. Your perspective may never or rarely ever get beyond the front lines. Wherever

> **WHEREVER YOU ARE IN THE ORGANIZATION, YOUR PERSPECTIVE IS UNIQUE. YOUR VANTAGE POINT CAN BE AN ADVANTAGE POINT.**

you are in the organization, your perspective is unique. Your vantage point can be an advantage point. Your location can provide perspective, pertinent information, cultural readings, problem-solving wisdom, and a sense of the emotional climate around you. Leading from the middle provides a particularly rich collection of perspectives for those who take the time to notice.

Advantageous Vantage

Second chair leaders have a fantastic vantage point, including contact with the first chair and the third chair. Such leaders can be connectors or conduits of the vision or communication from the first chair to all the other people downline. Because they are in the inner circle of the first chair leader's confidence, they typically have access to goals, vision, plans, and other

---

12   John Maxwell, *The 360 Degree Leader* (Nashville: Thomas Nelson Publishers, 2005).

communications well in advance of the other team players. They see before others see. Second chair leaders have an advantageous vantage point.

But, because of the proximity to the first chair leader, they also see more than most others see. While they are not sitting in first chair and don't necessarily have the complete picture in mind, they can see more clearly through the lens of the leader than most of the others on the team. Greater influence is often the result of closer proximity if the bond of trust between the first and second chair is robust.

Friendship

You can't delegate relationships. First-hand knowledge is different from common knowledge. Second chair leaders tend to know the leader in first chair better than those sitting farther down the positional line. They have the advantage of knowing not only the information but the man or woman sitting in the chair. They know them as people with feelings, opinions, and stories beyond the office walls and lines of authority. And, hopefully, they love, respect, and honor them as well. Most of all, second chair leaders understand that we are all people in process who are growing, changing, and transforming as we sharpen those around us as well as the leader inside us.

Second chair leaders have proximity or closeness to those in third chair as well. Because they are not in first chair, they are often perceived to be a bit more human or like all the other followers. They have proximity with the other's downline much more closely than the first chair leader. But they also have empathy for the leader in the first chair as well as all those in the chairs to the right. They get it. They understand. They feel the pain from both sides. They feel their pain in their own hearts. Someone defined empathy as the capacity for me to feel your pain in my heart. Second chair leaders can empathize with both the executives and those seated lower at the same time. And, because they are not sitting in first chair, they are perceived to be one of them. The followers.

As Campus Pastor at Emmanuel College, I had access to the President of the college. We met regularly to plan worship services, develop discipleship strategies, and orchestrate short-term missions domestically and internationally. But I also had access to the professors, students, staff members, and coaches as well. I worked closely with all the worship leaders and musicians, as well as any guests we sponsored on campus. Student ministry team leaders met regularly with me. Missions team sponsors met with me. Residence hall chaplains and their leadership teams met with me regularly. Since they had never had a campus pastor in the past, my life was full of meetings with people from every part of the college leadership community as well as the students and student leaders. It was my role to speak for the president and represent the values of the college publicly, but it was also my role to be the primary advocate for each constituency under the umbrella of spiritual life at the college. While I had no stated authority with the senior leadership team of the college, I had constant communication with most of them as well as weekly time with a wide representation of students and student leaders. Those friendships alone provided many opportunities for healthy influence from all sides.

Second chair leaders often have access and leverage. They have emotional and relational access to the heart but also physical access as well. But there is also the potential for substantial influence earned through faithful service and complete loyalty. Such esteem is also earned through honest appraisal and authentic relationships.

TRUST IS THE ONE THING THAT CHANGES EVERYTHING IN ORGANIZATIONS. WITHOUT IT, YOU CAN DO NOTHING

Of course, this leverage is ultimately earned through developing personal trust. And let me remind you that trust is the one thing that changes everything in organizations.[13] Without it, you can do nothing, but with real trust among leadership teams, the potential is almost unlimited.

Case Study: Moses & Aaron - 1st and 2nd Chair Leadership

"God told Moses, "Look at me. I'll make you as a god to Pharaoh, and your brother Aaron will be your prophet. You are to speak everything I command you, and your brother Aaron will tell it to Pharaoh. Then he will release the Israelites from his land. At the same time, I am going to put Pharaoh's back up and follow it up by filling Egypt with signs and wonders. Pharaoh is not going to listen to you, but I will have my way against Egypt and bring out my soldiers, my people, the Israelites, from Egypt by mighty acts of judgment. The Egyptians will realize that I am God when I step in and take

13   Stephen M.R. Covey, *The Speed of Trust* (New York: Simon & Schuster, Inc., 2006).

the Israelites out of their country." Moses and Aaron did exactly what God commanded. Moses was eighty and Aaron eighty-three when they spoke to Pharaoh. Then God spoke to Moses and Aaron. He said, "When Pharaoh speaks to you and says, 'Prove yourselves. Perform a miracle,' then tell Aaron, 'Take your staff and throw it down in front of Pharaoh: It will turn into a snake.'" Moses and Aaron went to Pharaoh and did what God commanded. Aaron threw his staff down in front of Pharaoh and his servants, and it turned into a snake. Pharaoh called in his wise men and sorcerers. The magicians of Egypt did the same thing by their spells: each man threw down his staff, and they all turned into snakes. But then Aaron's staff swallowed their staffs. Yet Pharaoh was as stubborn as ever—he wouldn't listen to them, just as God had said."

Aaron was three years older than Moses. But it was the younger brother, Moses, God chose to lead the people of Israel out of Egypt and into the promised land. God spoke to Moses directly through a strange burning bush that was not consumed by the fire. Yet, Moses was reluctant and lacked the confidence in himself to be the man God called him to be. He didn't see in himself the qualities he perceived necessary to do the work God had called him to do. On top of all that, Moses had a speech impediment akin to stuttering and felt unable to communicate clearly to the people and certainly not to Pharoah.

God even got angry with Moses for arguing with him and not complying readily by proposing alibis for why he was a poor choice as a deliverer. Therefore, God chose Aaron to be the right-hand man of Moses. God would speak to Moses, Moses would speak to Aaron, and Aaron would speak to the Pharoah. The right-hand man is code for second chair. God did not let Moses off the hook by using Aaron to lead Israel out of Egyptian bondage. Quite the contrary, Moses became the leader he was reluctant to be, but Aaron was the spokesperson to Pharoah. Also, Aaron was often the person who wielded the staff God used to perform miraculous signs before pharaoh and his magicians.

Moses and Aaron became a team. Nobody got them confused or reversed the roles God had given them by assignment. It was always Moses and Aaron, not Aaron and Moses. Wouldn't it be amazing what we could accomplish if we didn't care who got the credit? Aaron had a role, and Moses had a role, but God was the powerful force working the miracles and providing the proof that he was God of the universe calling his people out to the wilderness to worship him. It was a multi-step process of requests, denials, miracles, agreements, and changes of mind by the Pharoah before he was ready to release the people of Israel to worship their God in the wilderness.

Strike one was the Nile River turning into blood. Strike Two was a massive infestation of frogs. Strike three was an invasion of gnats. Strike four was flies. Strike five was the indiscriminate death of animals by disease while the animals of Israel thrived. Strike six was the sudden appearance of painful boils all over the bodies of the Egyptians. Strike Seven was a massive hailstorm destroying everything, including crops and animals. Strike eight was an infestation of locusts. Strike nine was a period of pitch darkness. Before the tenth plague, God warned a final time before all the firstborn sons of Egypt were killed. In each encounter, God orchestrated it all, Moses spoke for God to Pharoah, and Aaron did whatever he was told to do. They worked together with God.

What a picture of second chair leadership. One was not better than the other, nor was one chair more important than the other. Both were necessary to complete the mission. Each complimented the other. As they played their parts and fulfilled their roles, God worked through them, performing miraculous signs to his own glory. They had the same command and the same

> ONE WAS NOT BETTER THAN THE OTHER, NOR WAS ONE CHAIR MORE IMPORTANT THAN THE OTHER. BOTH WERE NECESSARY TO COMPLETE THE MISSION. EACH COMPLIMENTED THE OTHER.

communication. Both had access to God, but Moses spoke to God face-to-face, while Aaron depended on Moses to hear God speak. Scripture doesn't differentiate when Aaron was present and not present when God spoke. However, it was clear that they heard God, and they all worked together as a team. There was a first chair leader and a second chair leader. And there was Almighty God working through them both to achieve his purposes and receive the glory only He deserves.

I believe Moses was grateful for Aaron. I think Aaron made first chair leadership more enjoyable and less lonely for Moses. I believe Aaron was grateful for Moses. I think Aaron was glad Moses was Moses and he was not. I think Aaron appreciated and recognized the pressures Moses faced. And I think

Moses appreciated the support and encouragement Aaron provided. Two chairs. One team. One mission. One God. Mission accomplished.

Like Aaron, second chair leaders can accomplish amazing things when they move in concert with the leaders above them and below them. Vantage points afforded to second chair leaders can become advantage points for the organization if handled with integrity, effectiveness, and care.

Personal Reflection and Group Discussion

- Second chair provides multiple vantage points. What advantages have you discovered as you serve others above you, below you, and around you in your organization or team?

- Being in the middle brings a variety of pressures along with the location. What pressures have you experienced from those around you as a second chair leader?

- Access and proximity are often privileges experienced by second chair leaders. What kinds of pitfalls and temptations accompany this kind of trust? What safeguards do you recommend for those entrusted with greater access and closer proximity to all levels of the organization?

- In the case study of the two brothers, Moses and Aaron, where do you see the major points of tension and greatest opportunities for failure? Likewise, what were the keys to their success?

SECOND
CH■IR   7

Influencing From Second Chair

When asked the question, "Are you a leader or a follower?" many people would say they are not really leaders. They believe they are followers only. But consider this: the most introverted of people have been projected by social scientists to potentially influence upwards of 15,000 people in a 70-year lifespan. Whether you accept the title or position of leadership or not, we all have a sphere of influence. As we have already pointed out, leadership author and expert John Maxwell describes leadership as "influence...nothing more, nothing less."[14] Though I am not the chief leader or first chair player, I do have a responsibility to steward the leadership influence entrusted to me. Second chair leaders have tremendous opportunities to lead others within their sphere of influence.

Greener Grass Myth

Bloom where you are planted. Wherever you fall on the organizational chart, thrive, and serve extremely well. Turn the lemons into lemonade. Be the best version of yourself you can be. Lead faithfully, enthusiastically, and honorably right where you are. Don't try to kick down the doors or create a broader platform of opportunity. The writer of Psalm 75:6-7 informs us that, "No one from the ease or the west or from the desert can exalt themselves. It is God who judges: He brings one down, he exalts another." Rather than jockeying for position, accept your status and learn to thrive there. Flourish where you are. Don't be distracted by the opportunities afforded others but focus your energies on those right in front of you currently.

---

14   *Developing the Leader Within You*, 1.

Green grass is just that. The grass may be greener on the other side, but there are weeds on both sides. Everything is not always as it seems to be. Appearances can be deceptive and shallow. Erma Bombeck offered a better, more realistic perspective when she wrote, "The grass is always greener over the septic tank!"[15] Let's seize the opportunities afforded today and resist the temptation to worry about tomorrow, trusting that the grace of God will be sufficient to guide us and guard us into the future.

Develop Influence

Adding Value. One of the keys to developing influence is the continual practice of adding value. To add value is to help something improve. What might happen if we simply tried to make it a little better? We may not have the clout or the capital to make substantial improvements right now, but what if we just made it better? Solomon decried those little foxes as the varmints responsible for spoiling the vines, but what if we used our wits to devise small measures to keep the foxes out of the vineyard or at least slow them down? Rather than bemoaning the reality that we cannot solve world hunger or provide clean water for everyone by Friday at noon, what might be accomplished if we took the words of Andy Stanley to heart and simply, "Did for one what you wish you could do for everyone."[16] Add value. Make it better. Do for one. This may be the easiest and most effective way to increase influence over time.

And Then Some. Another means of developing influence is to live by the challenge contained in these three short words, "And then some." Do everything you are asked to do, and then some. And. Then. Some. It is not rocket science, brain surgery, or rocket surgery, but it is a proven method of self-improvement and sacrificial service when we exceed expectations. Great businesses have earned a competitive advantage by offering more than what was anticipated or expected by their customers. Customers become fans when we go the extra mile. Jesus didn't just turn the water into wine at the wedding at Cana; He put the wine served earlier to shame. The unsuspecting servant host accused the groom of saving the best wine for last, but it was actually Jesus who exceeded their expectations. And then some.

---

15   *The Grass is Always Greener Over the Septic Tank* (Greenwich: Fawcett Crest, 1972).
16   Andy Stanley, *Deep and Wide* (Grand Rapids: Zondervan, 2012) 78.

Take Initiative. Another means of increasing influence is to simply take initiative. Don't wait to be told or asked. Let the recognition of the need be the call to action. It has often been said that one characteristic of leadership is that the leaders go first. They take the plunge and are often the early adopters who initiate or embrace change. My wife, Lisa, has the primary love language of acts of service. I can tell her how much I love her multiple times per day, but she hears me much more clearly when my love for her is expressed in acts of service around the house. I daily try to take initiative and do small things around the house before being asked because I want Lisa to know how much I love her in ways she can recognize and appreciate. Don't wait or hesitate; simply take the next right step and do the next right thing.

Others-Centered Mindset. One sure way to increase your influence with others is to shift the focus away from yourself and onto others. Adopt an others-centered leadership mindset. Jesus took His cues from the needs of those around Him. If they were hungry, He fed them. If they were sick, He healed them. On a few occasions, He ever brought dead loved ones back to life. Scott Mautz characterizes others-centered leadership as "understanding and acting on the multitudes of perspectives you must consider when interacting up, down, and across your organization. If you want to thrive in leading from the middle, it can't be all about you. It's about helping everyone and everything around you to thrive. It's about the ecosystem, not the ego-system."[17]

Solve Problems. Finally, solve problems. That's what leaders do. I have long contended that any idiot can see a problem and call it out, but it takes a leader to do something about it and solve the problem! All vision begins as a problem to be solved that cannot be ignored and must be addressed. A vision is a preferred future or a future where the problem is solved by some means of intervention. Second

> ANY IDIOT CAN SEE A PROBLEM AND CALL IT OUT, BUT IT TAKES A LEADER TO DO SOMETHING ABOUT IT AND SOLVE THE PROBLEM!

chair leaders can increase their capacity to influence and grow their platform over time by adopting the mindset and skillset of solving problems on a regular basis. Become the go-to person. Find better solutions and commit to solving the problems rather than recognizing them or pointing them out.

17   *Leading From the Middle*, 27.

Leverage Up

Leverage your position by influencing up. Second chair leaders have access to first chair leaders. Become a caring and trusted friend to your first chair leaders. Show them honor and respect. Treat them kindly and personably. Take the time and energy to learn their story. Ask good questions and listen to their responses. Ask for their input and advice. When you don't understand, ask them to help you understand. Grant the benefit of the doubt. Assume the best about them. Learn the why behind their position. Seek to appreciate their point of view and look for common ground. As Steven Covey challenged us, "Seek first to understand, then to be understood."[18] Become a student of your first chair leader. The way to leverage those above you is to serve them by getting to know them and increasingly gaining an understanding of them.

Andy Stanley, a renowned first chair leader, says, "Loyalty publicly yields leverage privately." I know this to be true. I've had the privilege of working with some amazingly gifted and godly first chair leaders both in the church and in the academic arena. Perhaps it is in my genetics, but God has made me an extremely loyal follower of my leaders. You may criticize me, but you better not criticize my boss. I'm the same way with my teammates, my brothers, my wife, and my children. This comes naturally to me for some reason. I'm not looking for a pat on the back because it is much like breathing to me. I've always felt that if I could not be loyal to my leader that I should find another leader to serve whom I can place my utmost trust and loyalty. And, in the times when I have been tempted to be disloyal in even the smallest way, I have quickly realized that I either need to get a new attitude or a new address.

First Chair Relationship Pointers

Never waste your boss's time. Keep a list of things you need to discuss with them. Set up regular times to meet and always arrive early, have your list in hand, and don't waste their time. Never assume that you will have ample time with your first chair leader. That way, you will be ecstatic if they surprise you with more time together but not disappointed because they do not have the time to meet as much as you would like.

---

18   Stephen R. Covey, *The 7 Habits of Highly Effective People* (New York: Fireside, 1989) 237.

Maintain clarity by having your superiors choose your priorities. If you have ten things on the to-do list and don't have the time to do them all, ask your supervisor to choose the top three for now and rank order them for you in order of importance. This will assure that you will be working on the things they consider most important and should help you feel a bit less overwhelmed by all the things on your to-do list.

Don't engage in water cooler or breakroom conversations. If you must, avoid the water cooler or breakroom completely. Many organizations have places where naysayers gather, and negativism abounds. Don't frequent those places. And when those places or people come to you, either change the subject or change the tone by stating something positive about whoever or whatever they are harping on now. Send clear messages that you are not interested in those kinds of conversations and redirect the conversation around your positive experiences with that person if possible. If all else fails, simply walk away as soon as you can do so gracefully.

> MANY ORGANIZATIONS HAVE PLACES WHERE NAYSAYERS GATHER, AND NEGATIVISM ABOUNDS. DON'T FREQUENT THOSE PLACES.

Influence Around

Leverage your position by influencing around. In John Maxwell's book, *360 Degree Leadership*, he describes the idea of leading around you or leveraging your position by influencing others sitting in the same position or similar positions on the organizational chart.[19] Influence your colleagues. If you are a dean, influence the other deans. If you are an instructor, influence the other instructors. If you are an associate pastor, influence the other associate pastors. If you are a line worker, influence the other line workers. If you're a cashier, influence the other cashiers. If you are a line chef, influence the other line chefs. You get the picture. It may look like a positive attitude, excellent work ethic, positive results, personal support, or simple words of encouragement. But it can make all the difference in the lives of the other second chair leaders as well as the overall organization.

---

19   *The 360 Degree Leader, 159.*

BECOME A GOOD TEAMMATE. CARE ABOUT WHAT YOUR ASSOCIATES CARE ABOUT.

Become a good teammate. Care about what your associates care about. Meet them on their turf. Visit them in their office or workstation. Don't always insist that they come to you. Buy their coffee or pay for their lunch. Observe their favorite foods, beverages, desserts, candy bars, and snack foods, and surprise them with an unexpected gift periodically. Ask their opinion about issues like the ones you are facing in your area. Invite them to explain what they do and why they do it as the leader of their department or division. When you sense they need a word of encouragement, offer your words with sincerity. Learn about their family, how they met their spouse, what they enjoy doing together, other places they have lived, and future dreams or bucket lists they have. You may never become best friends but don't allow your relationship to become adversarial. As Paul challenged us, "As much as it depends on you, live at peace with all men" (Romans 12:18). Become an ally and a friend. Volunteer your help. Handle differences privately and as quickly as possible. Influence around.

Influencing Down

Leverage your position by influencing down. I hate the thought of anything being beneath you or me. So, we must fight the perception that anything would ever be beneath us because of our position, status, education, experience, or job description. Never ask people to do something you either have not done before or would not do again if given the opportunity. There's a tension here. I'm not saying you should spend most of your time doing things that fall into another person's job description, but I am saying that we need to see the playing field as perfectly leveled in our own minds and hearts. And we must routinely and regularly help others or, at the very least, offer to help them succeed. Help those you've enlisted to serve the meal by serving the meal yourself. Help those you've enlisted to set up the room by setting up the room with them, if even for just a few minutes. I would even encourage you to add at least one thing you do every week that others would think you don't need to do because we "pay other people to do that kind of thing." You may completely disagree with me, but I believe that one thing could be the very thing that builds stronger bonds and communicates the message that nothing is beneath you as you serve those entrusted to your care. People truly do not care how much you know until they know how much you care. Care about them. And act like you care about them.

It's a small thing. It usually takes me about half an hour each week.

But I think it sends the right kind of message, and it reminds me of who I am and that I am not above anything or anyone.

Every Thursday, I visit each small group room in our church to restock the coffee supplies, creamers, sweeteners, mints, chocolates, cups, lids, and bottled water we provide, along with a hand-delivered freshly brewed carafe of locally roasted medium roast coffee for their Sunday groups. Several times I have had other staff members remind me that I could get someone else to do that each week, but I try to be humble as I suggest to them that it is one little thing I can do to serve them each week and that it is actually therapeutic for me as it is one thing I can actually check off my to-do list when I am done. More importantly, I want them to know I appreciate them and see myself as a servant who provides everything I can to help them succeed and thrive. I need to be reminded.

Grow Them Intentionally

Make yourself available to your team. Make them your priority. Don't just develop yourself and your leadership; pass along what you are learning to them and learn with them. Teach them what you know and learn from them what they know. Make it your responsibility to grow them and create an environment where they can learn by doing, learn new things, and change old things. One of the reasons I provide a weekly podcast with my buddy, Chris Maxwell, is to provide great content to grow my own team and team leaders. Most weeks, I also send them a quick five-minute video with affirmations, informational updates, and quick tips or life hacks. To make sure I do not forget, I place it on my calendar each week and try not to miss even one week. Do it on purpose. Grow them intentionally.

> ONE OF THE SUREST WAYS TO FLATTEN THE ORGANIZATIONAL CHART IS TO EXPECT LEARNING TO OCCUR AT EVERY LEVEL.

Create a learning service culture. Be hungry to know and hungry to grow. One of the surest ways to flatten the organizational chart is to expect learning to occur at every level as we serve each other and the mission of the organization. Model the way by cultivating lifelong learning habits for yourself. Go to conferences regularly, attend webinars, listen to podcasts, read books, read articles, listen to audiobooks, and select mentors for yourself. Once you have established a pathway for yourself, take someone else along on the journey. Grow yourself and grow them too. Intentionally.

Personal Reflection and Group Discussion

- Do you consider yourself more of a leader or a follower? In what situations are you more likely to lead? Conversely, in what situations are you more likely to follow?

- Learning to be content is vital to sustainable satisfaction. In what areas do you fight discontent? How are you learning to 'bloom where you are planted' and find contentment currently?

- Tracy lists several ways to gain influence in organizations:
  o Adding value
  o And then some
  o Taking initiative
  o Others-centered mindset
  o Problem-solving

- Think of times or situations where you have done each of these well. How do you think these types of behaviors and mindsets can increase potential influence for any leader?

- Because second chair leaders are positioned between those above them, around them, and below them on the organizational flow chart, our influence is required in every direction and from every angle. What suggestions or practices would you suggest that might enhance your influence above, around, and below?

Creating From Second Chair

One advantage of sitting in second chair is that you are situated a bit closer to the problems at hand and can potentially have a more active role in solving them. Granted, there are many ways to solve a problem. But there is a heightened opportunity to exercise creativity and create novelty in organizations when you sit in second chair.

Mike Bonem & Roger Patterson suggest that second chair leaders operate regularly in the "deep and wide paradox." "They have no choice. Their role requires them to see the big picture and make decisions that affect the entire organization. It frequently requires them to delve into the details to solve a problem in some part of the organization, or to launch a new ministry."[20] As such, they challenge second chair leaders to become pulse takers who understand more deeply what others are thinking and feeling; vision amplifiers who constantly repeat, explain, and bring clarity around the organizational vision; leader multipliers who constantly empower others in leadership capacities; and gap fillers who can serve at a moment's notice in important roles in due season. Both dimensions, depth, and breadth, are crucial to effective leadership and problem-solving at the second chair level of service.

Problem Solvers and Vision Implementers

Second chair leaders are afforded wonderful opportunities to be problem solvers and vision implementers. Since it is not their normal lot to create the vision or dream about preferred futures, second chair leaders take up the mantle of strategic thinking, creative solutions to complex problems, and game plans to move the organization toward the accomplishment of its mission. Strategies and game plans are the bread and butter of their existence.

20   *Leading From the Second Chair*, 67.

At least one thing we have learned from our GPS Google Maps is that there are many ways to move from one point on the planet to another. There are alternate routes. Even Google Maps knows to avoid traffic at certain times of day and will guide you around accidents, major delays, and construction sometimes. Well, maybe not construction so much. There have been times when I wanted to punch the programmers at Google Maps as they seemed innocuous to road construction! There are other times when I purposely get off the beaten path and engage Google Maps just to find a novel way to get home. At those times, finding a new path forward is exhilarating and fun. Brainstorming solutions and solving old problems with novel methods is much akin to Google Maps in that regard. **Someone else picks the destination; second chair leaders find creative, strategic ways to get there.**

> SECOND CHAIR LEADERS HAVE A BETTER VANTAGE POINT THAN FIRST CHAIR LEADERS TO RECRUIT AND INSPIRE THE BEST POTENTIAL PROBLEM SOLVERS TO THE TEAM.

Creative problem-solving is the fastest way I know to generate trust and begin building momentum. Second chair leaders have a better vantage point than first chair leaders to recruit and inspire the best potential problem solvers to the team. They can provide opportunities for creative input, allow for greater risk without fear of failure or punishment, and absorb the shock when something doesn't go according to plan. Second chair leaders have the capability to empower and unleash the energy to imagine creative solutions.

Innovative Breakthroughs

First chair leaders love it when second chair leaders take something significant off their plate of responsibilities and handle it for them with excellence and creative brilliance. Everybody wins, and morale rises. You make the boss's job easier and a bit better, you solve a problem they don't have time to address, and you add value to them and their organization. It is a win-win-win!

Be warned, however. You might want to prepare yourself to never receive credit for those revolutionary successes…or at least not receive full credit. There are numerous times in the life of a second chair leader when the first chair receives glory, adulation, and praise for the work you and your team invest in the project. Your team makes them look good or better than they are. However, I would be quick to add that it should never have been about credit in the first place. But it's best to warn you so you can be prepared to celebrate privately with your teams when it happens to you. We will spend more time on this in the later chapter on second chair failure and fatal flaws.

Solving Problems At The Lowest Levels

I've always believed that problems should be solved at the lowest possible level in the organization. This is yet another fitting application of Jethro's helpful advice to Moses, discussed in the last chapter. Like Moses was instructed by Jethro to divide his responsibilities and empower others to solve the issues from the ordinary everyday lives of the Israelites, second chair leaders also have continual opportunities presented to them where empowerment of people on the front line, at the front desk, on the bottom floor, and at the lowest ranks is possible and preferable.

But how can we empower those at the lowest levels of the organization to be creative thinkers and problem solvers? Ask questions. Ask the person bringing the problem to your attention what they think. Listen to their answers. Follow up their answers with questions delving a bit deeper into the matter at hand. Again, listen well and hear their rationale. Their answer will likely not always be the right or best answer, but it will usually be an answer worth hearing and sometimes worth testing. Asking and listening, then asking and listening again, creates opportunities for second chair leaders to give the grass-roots solutions of those they lead genuine consideration and perhaps a trial run, even if just for a short season.

How do you think someone on the front lines might feel if you not only listened to their solutions but put them into practice? Even if they had to be changed later or tweaked a bit, the net gains to your organization will likely pay greater dividends in the long run than any short-term losses incurred. And remember, what you are currently doing isn't working anyway! What have you got to lose? The increase in morale generated by sincere interest, attentive listening, and serious consideration can be palpable.

During my tenure as vice president of student development at the college, I was overwhelmed with the inquiries we were constantly receiving around issues involving practical challenges related to housing, service animals, students with allergies, and the tensions of compliance with federal regulations. The person I most often engaged in this area worked with students, parents, resident assistants, and the director of residence life. She had the wisdom, experience, and emotional intelligence to handle complaints, solve problems, and work with others, but she did not have the title or position required. I will never forget the meeting where I asked her to take on these responsibilities, report directly to me, and receive both a raise, authority increase and change of title. All she needed was someone to believe that she could do it, and we both cried as she accepted the changes at our meeting the next day. She proved her value within the first few days of her new role, and we got better solutions and happier team members, students, parents, and administrators. All I had to do was get out of the way and believe she could do it.

Letting Them Figure It Out

> ONE OF MY FAVORITE LINES I LOVE SHARING WITH PEOPLE I OVERSEE IS THE SIMPLE AFFIRMATION, "YOU'LL FIGURE IT OUT!"

One of my favorite lines I love sharing with people on teams I oversee is the simple affirmation, "You'll figure it out!" In my experience, that affirmation does at least a couple of helpful things. First, it highlights my belief in that person and their ability. While they may not want to hear it and may feel uncomfortable with the weight of the responsibility, I'm betting that it is nice to know someone thinks you can do it. Second, it places the ball back in their court and moves the ownership back to them. I am communicating that I trust them and need them to take the matter into their hands and solve the problem at hand.

But then you must let them figure it out. And you cannot criticize their efforts if they fall short. You may have to reinsert yourself, however, at various points in the process. But see yourself as more of a coach than a player and more of a consultant than a boss. Very few things build trust better or more quickly than granting trust and empowering teams to solve problems using their own creativity and abilities. Once again, everybody wins. And a rising tide lifts all the boats!

Personal Reflection and Group Discussion

Bonem & Patterson introduce the "deep and wide paradox" where second chair leaders must focus on the big picture while delving into the myriad of details. How have you experienced the tension of depth and breadth in your leadership?

- Do you consider yourself more of a big-picture person, a detail-oriented person, or a combination of both? Do you spend most of your time painting the big-picture vision for your team or helping them connect the dots or sort through the weeds around current problems being addressed?

- How do you suggest second chair leaders push the problems down to the lowest levels of the organization or team? What kinds of systems are needed to gain the input of those closest to the problems?

- How are problem-solvers and innovators rewarded? What kinds of things motivate and encourage them? Are there any barriers that need to be removed to help you encourage or reward them?

SECOND CHAIR

9

Peacemaking From Second Chair

Andy Stanley once said, "Loyalty publicly yields leverage privately." Public support encourages potential private influence. I have personally experienced the benefit and blessing of this statement. During my professional career in local church ministry, I have been privileged to serve some amazing and capable leaders. Examples include Larry Timmerman, Bennie S. Triplett, David Cooper, Mike Atkins, and Tony Vismor. All are wonderful leaders who have gained my implicit trust through the years. Their integrity and selfless service made it easy to follow, support, and endorse both publicly and privately. I've had many, many opportunities to prove my loyalty to them in public and privately. However, I have also had opportunities where I could have been disloyal, divisive, or damaging to the trust among our people. Call me old-fashioned, but loyalty to my first chair is an important value to me.

We have all seen the devastation of disloyalty in organizations. From my house to the White House, we are painfully aware of all that hangs in the balance when a trusted leader chooses self-interest and self-serving purpose over the greater needs of the family, church, business, or government. If malice, greed, envy, or vengeance is allowed to captivate the heart of second chair leaders, the destruction can be pervasive and virtually irreparable. Please do not misunderstand me; there are situations that warrant blowing the whistle and caring enough to confront wrong attitudes and actions within organizations. I am not talking about blind trust or unhealthy denial. Rather, I am speaking of a commitment to the first chair leader and the organization that is characterized by peace-making rather than troublemaking. And the peace I am speaking about is far more than the absence of war.

One of the greatest services exemplary second chair leaders can provide their organization is the service of peacemaking.

The Comparison Trap

One of the temptations often faced by second chair leaders is unique and not as obvious as you might think. When given the opportunity to speak in their stead at their invitation or to lead in their absence in almost any capacity, it is not unusual for a well-meaning or less-than-noble member of the organization to tempt the young associate by lavishing them with praise or even imply that they would rather hear you than your boss, the first chair leader. In those moments, what comes out of our mouths next may prove to be some of the most important words we will ever speak.

> I HAVE LEARNED TO VIEW THIS AS A TEST AND TEMPTATION TO BE HANDLED WITH GRACE, GRATITUDE, AND A DECISIVE VOTE OF SUPPORT TO MY FIRST CHAIR LEADER.

We have an opportunity to affirm our leaders and our complete loyalty to them. Or, we have an opportunity to graciously receive their praise, mull over it, and talk ourselves into believing it to be true. Over the years, I have learned to view this as a test and temptation to be handled with grace, gratitude, and a decisive vote of support to my senior, first chair leader. After all, he trusted me to speak or lead in his stead. My response to their praise? "Thank you for your encouragement. You're very kind. I can only imagine how our pastor preaches so effectively week after week for years with only days to prepare. I had six months to prepare and absolutely no excuse if I had handled it poorly! I thank God for our pastor, don't you?"

Before you label me a suck-up, please allow me to unpack that response a bit. I believe most people who say those encouraging overstatements about our performances mean well. At the same time, there are some exceptions to the rule. Most of those folks simply want to encourage us. So, thank them for their encouragement. I really do appreciate it. My affirmation of their kindness moves the focus away from me and acknowledges their gesture while providing space to redirect their thoughts and change the subject instead of encouraging them to tell us more about how great I am. And the statements about how hard it is to hit a grand slam home run every time the pastor gives a weekly message is mostly for my benefit, lest I forget how easy a one-off is to pull off when we don't have to perform repeatedly at that level of expectation. At the end of the day, I was loyally affirmed, and I don't feel guilty for stealing anybody's ego food. That kind of comparison is a trap. See it for what it could be and step over it rather than stepping into it.

Peace in The Midst Of Storms

The comparison trap is an example of peacemaking before there was a true conflict. Unfortunately, there are numerous examples in scripture where second chair leaders tried to usurp the authority of the first chair leader. My mind races to Absalom, the son of King David, who deceptively won the hearts of the people by standing at the gates and listening to their problems ever so disingenuously pretending he cared when all the time it was a ploy to steal the throne from his dad. Even Miriam, the sister of Moses, and Aaron, his brother, struggled when tempted to take control when Moses was off doing his duty before God. After all, Moses couldn't complete a sentence while Aaron was Ronald Reagan and Miriam was the likely next contestant on The Voice.

Insubordination happens. Disloyalty happens. Often, as in the biblical stories above, that insubordinate disloyalty is both misguided and entirely without cause. Sometimes, however, the disloyalty can be misguided even while having a just cause. For instance, occasionally, a great second chair leader can be positioned underneath a truly bad first chair, and others in the organization have noticed and may even be suffering for it. In that case, how do you stay humble and satisfied when it is obvious to most that you are the better leader, the preferred speaker, or the long-awaited messiah? If given the opportunity, most of us can become legends in our own minds. How do you keep the peace when the storms are real, and the battles are raging?

Ironically, one of the best examples in the entirety of scripture is King David himself, who avoided conflict with his master, King Saul, on many occasions. David ran away from the conflict before anyone fully recognized there was an actual problem. Nobody wanted to believe that the king was trying to kill him out of jealousy during fits of rage in the palace. Even David's best friend, Jonathan, argued with David on this one. The irony is that David was employed by the king to play the harp to soothe and calm him down when he had these outrageous fits of anger. And David consulted with Jonathan to confirm his suspicions, and both agreed the best strategy would be for David to exit the palace and run away from the conflict.

David did not gather his loyal friends and stage a coup. He didn't serve a two-week notice or give any sort of warning. He left quietly. There was no defensive posturing or fighting back. David left before things got worse.

Sometimes our best choice is to leave quietly even though we are in the right and everyone on the team knows it is true. Your presence there may be the one thing keeping your leader from facing their demons and learning from the situation. Rather than debates and divisions, what if you just left quietly and said nothing? David did.

But Saul was relentless and driven to eliminate the threat David posed in his twisted thoughts. Saul put together a posse of his best soldiers and declared a full-on manhunt. David had every justification to fight back and rally the people to overthrow the king, but it never happened. Not once. Twice, David was given the opportunity to avenge himself against the king by taking his life himself or allowing one of his servants to do so. David would not touch the man God had anointed king even though David himself had been anointed the next king of Israel by the prophet Samuel. He would not promote himself, and he would not permit those around him to do so, either. If he would be King, it would be because God clearly placed him there and not he himself. In both instances, peace was established and maintained. David provides ample examples of peacemaking from second chair long before he was promoted to first chair.

Everyday Conflicts

While those examples are both insidious and covert, perhaps the more common opportunities for peacemaking are found in the instances when we help people deal with their differences, mediate their controversies, and maintain the peace between staff members, teammates, and even family members in our homes. I call those "basic Bb conflicts." These are the ordinary everyday opportunities every second chair leader encounters with great regularity. Romans 12:18 challenges me every second of every day. "If it is possible, as far as it depends on you, live at peace with everyone." I believe second chair leaders have more opportunities to live up to the peacemaking challenge than anyone in the organization. Everyday conflicts provide everyday opportunities for us to be the chief peacemakers.

EVERYDAY CONFLICTS PROVIDE EVERYDAY OPPORTUNITIES FOR US TO BE THE CHIEF PEACEMAKERS.

In healthy organizations, people tend to be positive and speak positively about each other. Positivity is the norm. Negativity feels out of place. Cynicism and skepticism are met with hopefulness and aspiration. Failure is a chance to do things better the next time and learn from our mistakes. Problems are viewed as opportunities to be ceased rather than threats to be avoided. Criticism is framed as coaching. Faults are not hidden but acknowledged, and grace is granted mutually towards the growth and development of each person on the team. Risk is welcomed, and change is the vehicle for accomplishment. Seeking to understand each other is more important than seeking to be understood. Apathy, stagnation, drifting, and the status quo are enemies of the state in a healthy organization. These organizations are full of conflicting opinions and ways of doing things, but the mission and vision of the collective trumps pettiness and siloed thinking. The energy and inertia of positivity build trust, confidence, and peacefulness among the ranks. And the leaders in the second chair are the purveyors of peacemaking throughout the organization.

Be Careful Little Mouth What You Say

Messaging matters. Content is important. Words carry meaning. Choosing the right words to communicate our message is worth the time to get it right the first time. Like my Dad says, "There's never enough time to do it right, but always enough time to do it over!" Psychologists and counselors have pushed us to communicate with "I" messages rather than the impulsive finger-pointing of "You" messages. The truth is that you do not make me mad. Your actions or attitudes may help me choose anger as my emotional climate of the minute, but you did not make me choose anger. That honor is all mine and not yours. Far better for me to openly confess that when you say things, do things, or use that tone, I feel belittled, taken for granted, or ignorant is a far better means of expressing both my feelings and my interpretation of your part of the story.

You may remember that children's song, "Be Careful Little Mouth What You Say," from children's church or preschool. The message of the song was a reminder to all the little people that words matter. Sticks and stones may break bones, but words can crush our spirit. Peacemakers constantly keep a close watch over their mouths and the words that tend to proceed out of them. Multiple times per day, second chair leaders have opportunities to communicate messages. We articulate and amplify the vision and goals of first chair leaders. We interpret and smooth over misunderstandings, often stoked by harsh or insensitive messages. We constantly choose the best methods of communicating the message or tailor the mode to fit several different modalities of our teammates or parishioners. A timely word, well-spoken, is priceless in value. A misplaced or misguided word can be like a heat-seeking missile scattering shrapnel in every direction. We must give careful thought to our choice of words. We must massage our messaging.

How You Say It, How You Do It

EVEN WHEN YOU'VE GOT THE RIGHT MESSAGE, *HOW* YOU SAY WHAT YOU SAY CAN TRUMP OR CANCEL THE BENEFIT OF THE MESSAGE ITSELF.

Maybe you are like me and my Daddy? Often it wasn't what we said but the way we said it that created the fallout. When that happened, our relationship became an illustration of the unfortunate yet true principle that sometimes the method becomes the message. A text message rather than an email or an email rather than a phone call or a phone call rather than a face-to-face conversation derailed the meaning of the message we were striving to communicate. Even when you've got the right message, *how* you say what you say can often trump or cancel the benefit of the message itself, inviting misunderstandings, misinterpretations, and exaggerated reactions rather than appropriate responses. Delivery and delivery systems require wisdom, reflection, and thoughtfulness. Blurting causes hurting. Blabber makes them madder.

Musically, you can play all the right notes, rhythms, dynamics, phrasing, and tempo while being horrifically out of tune with everyone else to the point that no one notices the beauty. Your message is wasted and misunderstood. What should have been gorgeous and inspiring hurt our ears and furrowed our brows. What could have been awesome became awful instead.

Organizational cultures that are negative and trending toward toxicity tend to communicate poorly. Even their best messages are communicated poorly. Private conversations and gossip demean the way things are handled and the way things are communicated. The benefit of the doubt is not normally granted. Assumptions are negative. Trust levels are low. Much of this could have been avoided if we had taken the time to carefully align both the message and the messaging methods beforehand. And do not underestimate the value of asking other trusted second chair folks for their take on things before going public with the information.

What we say and how we say it are key considerations for second chair leaders seeking to be peacekeepers.

Personal Reflection and Group Discussion

- Andy Stanley said, "Loyalty publicly yields leverage privately." Have you found this to be true? Would you agree that those who prove themselves loyal to you publicly are granted greater access and more serious consideration privately as well?

- What are some of the best ways you have learned to handle conversations where others compare you and your first chair leader? How have you handled it well and not so well?

- Peacemaking is not a denial of a genuine problem or avoidance of a real issue. What kind of thresholds or trigger points necessitate reporting a problem or exposing an issue in your organization? Do you know who you should report to and how you should report it?

- As King David experienced, there are times when we cannot control what the first chair leader does or how they do it, but we can control our response. What kinds of safeguards should we have in place to help us make the right decisions daily?

SECOND CHAIR 10

Advocating From Second Chair

An advocate is someone who speaks or writes in support or defense of a person or cause. Whether in prayer closets, conference rooms, or courthouses, advocates make it their mission to plead the case of another person, interceding especially on behalf of those who lack the power or clout to stand up for themselves. Advocates are backers, campaigners, defenders, lawyers, promoters, proponents, and supporters. Second chair leaders continually have opportunities to advocate for others who might otherwise remain silent or have no voice.

John Maxwell said it well, "The people at the bottom can see and understand things on their own level and, if they're perceptive, also on yours. The people at the top can see and understand things on their own level and on one below theirs, which would be yours. But as a leader in the middle, you should be able to see and understand not only things on your own level but also one level up and one level down. That gives you a really unique advantage and opportunity."[21] Rather than feeling like we are caught in the middle or stuck in the middle, second chair leaders should embrace their uniquely rare perspective, advantage, and opportunity to influence and advocate in all directions.

The Advantage of Proximity

I believe the best person to try solving an issue or problem is the person closest to the problem. The front-line worker is the best person to solve a front-line issue. The person working in the shoe department is the best person to solve an issue in the shoe department. The person closest to the problem will

---

21   *The 360 Degree Leader*, 287.

better understand the nature of the problem. They have clearer perspective, particularly as it relates to the customer or stakeholders in the organization. They understand the nuances of the situation and are more likely to possess insight as to the root causes and related issues. The farther removed we are from any situation, the less likely we will be able to understand the perspective and the nature of the issues surrounding that situation.

Wise leaders listen to those leading from chairs closer to the problem. Thus, the people sitting in those chairs become advocates for the needs, wants, and issues relevant and prevalent to those further down the organizational chart. Second chair leaders become vital communicators to the leader and for the leader. They are expected to perceive and communicate, when necessary, on behalf of those who will likely not have access to first chair leaders. And they are trusted to do so clearly and passionately. On the other hand, they are equally expected to represent the first chair leader to those on or closer to the front-line issues. There is a double-edged trust implicit in second chair leadership. Likewise, there is a double-edged responsibility as well. Accurate understanding and clear communication are vital if issues are to be understood and handled effectively and efficiently.

Empathy in Advocacy

> **EMPATHY IS A PREREQUISITE FOR EFFECTIVE ADVOCACY.**

In the arena of church leadership, the student pastor is the primary communicator to senior leadership regarding the needs, wants, and desires of the students they serve. The student pastor must be close enough to the students to feel their pain, sense their burdens, and understand the challenges they face. They must be empathetic to understand and reflect the pain felt by the students they serve. Empathy is a word used to describe the process of feeling the pain of another in our own hearts. It is entering into the world of another to relate, perceive, and understand more fully what life is like in their shoes and from their perspective. Empathy is a prerequisite for effective advocacy. We must care enough to move beyond knowing to feel the pain of the other person individually and specifically.

Empathy is rarely accidental. It requires intentionality, time, quiet reflection, and a desire to understand. To see what they see, I need to stand more closely to where they stand. Proximity precedes empathy. Without proximity, empathy could be little more than sympathy. More times than not, others do not want your sympathy but cherish being better understood and fully appreciated. What does it feel like to be them? How must it feel to face things from their unique circumstances? The ears of the second chair leader become the primary pathway to the heart. And the heart, deeply moved, cannot help but speak up for those whose needs we now feel. For second chair leaders, empathy becomes the necessary and best fuel for well-articulated, passionate advocacy.

Because of their clearer perspective of organizational reality and deeper understanding of the complexity around organizational challenges, the second chair leader has the task of promoting the causes, communicating the concerns, and balancing the weight of the particular and unique needs of the student ministry considering the more global and comprehensive conditions of the larger organization. The counterbalance of current organizational reality with the specific current dilemma facing the students in our student ministry helps us to consider more realistically what we can begin to address now, what we cannot address currently, and anticipate where we should temper our expectations considering where things currently stand in the larger organization. Simple, huh?

Double-Sided Messaging

Second chair leaders must speak from both sides of their mouth. They must speak eloquently, passionately, and accurately as advocates for all things related to student ministry, but they must also speak honestly, lovingly, and hopefully to

> SECOND CHAIR LEADERS LIVE IN THE TENSION BETWEEN SPEAKING UP FOR AND SPEAKING DOWN TO.

those students and student leaders regarding the current conditions, organizational climate, and genuine care of the compassionate first chair leaders. Second chair leaders live in the tension between speaking up for and speaking down to. Like skilled translators of foreign languages, second chair leaders must choose their words wisely and shape their messaging accordingly.

Those you serve fully expect you to speak up loudly and clearly for their concerns. They may not understand the need to choose the right time to speak and the right time to remain silent. They may not understand that you must choose your battles wisely and prioritize their concerns considering the larger concerns facing the organization. If their concern correlates and lines up with the mission, vision, and values of the organization, then it will be much easier to share and more likely to garner support. But if the current concerns from the lower positions are not even on the radar screen or seem irrelevant to the larger needs of the organization currently, sharing those concerns could work against any feelings of support or understanding by the first chair leaders. Second chair leaders need discernment to choose wisely in such cases. If that seems a bit squishy and intuitive, so be it. Only short-sighted leaders lacking any true sense of intuition would dare call it the "soft side" of leadership.

The Other Side of Advocacy Coin

But that is only one side of the responsibility given to a second chair leader serving as an advocate. The other half is the communication back to the constituents. First chair leaders expect and deserve loyalty from second chair leaders. First-person plural pronouns are critical and vital when communicating back to our constituents. They, them, and their should not be part of your vocabulary. We and our are better choices simply because they imply ownership and participation. Those kinds of words also communicate agreement and endorsement even when the decision or judgment is not favorable or does not feel much like support to those we serve. Never throw either side under the bus. Think those thoughts if you must but walk out of the room before you utter those words.

I like to think of these kinds of organizational tensions much like I think of prayer. When we approach God regarding any issue, the answer can be one of three things: yes, no, or wait. Chances are we're not going to like two of those three responses. It's the same with organizations.

Personal Reflection and Group Discussion

- When you think of an advocate, what thoughts or images come to mind? Have you ever had anyone speak up for you or support you in a meaningful way when you were not able to do so yourself? What was that like?

- What prevents some first chair leaders from empowering those on the front line to make decisions?

  o If you have ever served an organization where you felt empowered and trusted to make decisions, think about how that made you feel. Describe the team dynamics you experienced.

  o If you have ever served an organization where you did not feel empowered and trusted to make decisions, thank about how that made you feel. What emotions did you experience during that time?

- Describe the differences between sympathy and empathy. Tracy says, "Empathy becomes the necessary and best fuel for well-articulated, passionate advocacy." Many disagree and claim empathy as a 'soft skill' or less important to effective leadership. What do you think?

- "Second chair leaders live in the tension between speaking up for and speaking down to. Like skilled translators of foreign language, second chair leaders must choose their words wisely and shape their messaging accordingly." In what ways do second chair leaders act as filters and conduits regarding messaging up and down the organizational flow of communication? How would you advise second chair leaders desiring to say the right things at the right time in the right way for the right reasons?

SECOND CHAIR

11

Supporting From Second Chair

Larry Timmerman. Benny Triplett. David Cooper. Terry Ross. Jim Burkett. Mike Atkins. Jeris Hayes. David Hopkins. Paul Oxley. Earl Beatty. Tim Harrison. Kent Wessinger. Regina Moon. Michael Quick. Mike Luper. Mike Stewart. Craig Edwards. Tony Vismor. John Henzel. Ron White. Josh Rice.

What do all these names have in common?

All of them were my bosses at one time or another in the past 40+ years. I've been privileged to serve alongside some wonderfully amazing leaders, pastors, educators, administrators, presidents, vice presidents, deans, senior pastors, and lead pastors. As a second chair leader, I offered them my full support.

Support is different from loyalty. The heart of loyalty is faithfulness. Loyalty is exhibited by showing faithfulness to commitments, vows, obligations, positions, and people. It is a disposition staked upon a chosen commitment. Support implies coming alongside to support, bear up, or hold up the cause of another. Financial support requires us to invest our personal treasure to provide the means necessary for some cause, person, or organization to exist. Physical support implies the provision of support, balance, and undergirding needed to sustain or withstand someone who is under duress or pressure. In addition to loyalty, second chair leaders have both the opportunity and obligation to support our organization and its first chair leaders.

Different Strokes, Different Folks

As I read over the list of leaders above, I am immediately reminded why I followed their lead and chose to come alongside to help them accomplish the mission we shared. Some were great preachers. Others were true statesmen and ambassadors for the Kingdom of God. Many are excellent communicators who communicate truth and powerful messages effectively. Some were charismatic, and, like the Pied Piper of Hamlin, people lined up behind them because of their confidence and clear direction. A couple turned out to be more like wolves in sheep's clothing or rose to the level of their own incompetence. Many of them expressed strong belief in me. All of them supported me and encouraged me. Some were spiritual mentors and life coaches. A few were great at starting things, apostolic and bold, but were deeply challenged to complete projects. Some were "people people" and deeply pastoral in their style. A few were autocratic more than democratic, leading from the top down rather than empowering the team. Most, however, lead using teams to invigorate, create, shape, develop, and deploy both their talents and our well-developed plans. Some were academic, but all were educated.

I loved and admired them all. They weren't equally gifted and led from a variety of different styles. Not all were effective, and some were simply inefficient. I worked with some for longer periods of time and wonderful tenures, while others lasted one or two years. I appreciated the opportunity to serve with them and gave them my full support. I would hope if given the opportunity, they would hire me again or recommend me to you. I sat in second chair while they sat in first. Today I honor them and thank God for the privilege of coming along beside them for the season of my life and theirs. I am indebted for all I have learned from them. Mostly I'm grateful. And for the most part, I have no regrets.

Called Alongside to Help

I believe a prerequisite for following a leader is identification with their mission, vision, and values. We must care deeply about the problem they are trying to solve. We must identify with and buy into their vision to change the status quo to a preferred future. We must be convinced to the extent that we get on the bus, find our seats on the bus, and share the journey as partners. The first step of support is belief in the cause and desire to help.

I've always identified with the Greek word often used to denote the Holy Spirit in the New Testament, paraclete. My personal favorite definition is, "one called alongside to help." In my estimation, that's the first and foremost task of second chair leaders. As men and women occupying second chair positions, we are called, designated, summoned, assigned, chosen, selected, hired, beckoned, drawn, motivated, inspired, moved, compelled, convicted, honored, destined, and moved to join the ranks and come alongside to help the team achieve the mission, calling, and purpose of our organization. Other than that, I do not have an opinion.

We resonate with the need. We align with the values. We embrace the vision. We believe in the work. We invest with our belief, our time, and our treasure. We commit to come alongside. We support the leader by supporting the causes endorsed and championed by the organization. We commit to help. We trust the leader. Trust is where it all begins or ends.

The One Thing That Changes Everything

A prerequisite for supporting any leader is basic trust. I'm not talking about some esoteric emotional feeling or squishy generalized belief. Trust is based on evidence and experience as well as perception over time. We can-

> WE CANNOT DEMAND OR FORCE OTHERS TO TRUST US. TRUST IS EARNED.

not demand or force others to trust us. Trust is earned. Trust can be granted and later withdrawn. Trust is earned regularly and repeatedly. Levels and degrees of trust rise and fall precipitously based on decisions made, judgments rendered, and choices chosen over time.

John Maxwell made the concept of pocket change popular as it relates to how we earn and leverage trust in organizations and relationships.[22] At the beginning of each relationship, we tend to extend a measure of pocket change or trust to each other. That change serves as a deposit into our relational bank accounts. We tend to keep accounts on each other as we experience life together on teams and with organizations we serve. If we make consistently good choices over time, people grant us more trust and our trust deposits increase in value. We have earned a bit more trust or relational

---

22   John Maxwell, *The 21 Irrefutable Laws of Leadership* (Nashville: Thomas Nelson, 1998) 57.

pocket change. If we make a great decision and everyone seems to benefit, our trust may balloon, and trust accounts soar exponentially. With time and consistently solid wise choices observed by others, our trust interest compounds almost daily.

However, if we make poor decisions and exercise bad judgment in the eyes of those in our sphere of influence, our trust values take a hit and decrease. The larger the magnitude of the decision, the greater the trust deficit experienced. Trust is fluid rather than static. It fluctuates much like the stock market values based on performance, wisdom, equity, fairness, and justice. And let's not forget the role of perception in the accumulation or decimation of pocket change trust. Right decisions communicated poorly lead to declining trust account balances. The right thing done at the wrong time can also hurt our trust levels. Being associated with certain people or groups of people can lead to changes in our trust bank accounts. But the wrong decision made at the wrong time can yield devastating results to our trust bank accounts. It's complicated. It's never-ending. As I said before, trust is verified and earned almost by the hour in the 21st-century climate of litigation, cancellation, and polarization.

> **PEOPLE DON'T ENDORSE PRODUCTS OR PEOPLE THEY DO NOT TRUST. ONCE TRUST IS VIOLATED, THE JOURNEY IS LONG, TEDIOUSLY SLOW, AND COMPLICATED TO REBUILD.**

We follow people we trust. Trust, as Steven M.R. Covey has stated, is "the one thing that changes everything" as it relates to relationships and organizational health.[23] A lack of trust in leaders and organizations slows things down, causing greater expense and loss of revenue to the organization. People hesitate to sign up for support or volunteer to serve. Consequently, people lower their investment and decrease their commitment as they wait to see if things improve or decline. **People don't endorse products or people they do not trust. And, once trust is violated, the journey is long, tediously slow, and complicated to rebuild and regain trust.** Some people are simply out and will never come back. They renege on their commitments. They pull their money out or vote with their voice, their time, or their feet. If there is no trust, there is no leadership. Leadership moves at the speed of trust.

23   Stephen M.R. Covey, *The Speed of Trust* (New York: Free Press, 2006).

Trust Granted

Second chair support tends to correlate closely with the trust of the person sitting in first chair. In Jim Collins' classic, *Good To* Great, the most trusted and reliable leaders in the most prestigious companies globally are called Level Five leaders.[24] Level Five Leaders are characterized as trustworthy primarily and essentially. We support people we trust. We believe in the competence, character, and chemistry displayed and experienced together. We believe that the leader has the best interests of the organization in mind. We also believe that they place the needs of others before and above their own personal or selfish needs. We observe the sacrifice of their time, energy, and hours of effort to accomplish the mission we are commissioned to carry out. Finally, we sense their trust in us and confidence in our capacity to add value to the team and the organization as well as the mission.

People we trust deeply seem to receive increasingly higher levels of trust from us the closer we get to them. However, sometimes the inverse or opposite is true, and the closer we get to them, the less we trust them. We perceive inequity and a lack of authenticity; thus, we trust them less than we did before this realization. When there is a lack of alignment between what they say and what they do, trust wanes. When you don't have trust, you don't have influence. When you don't have influence, you don't have leadership. Support from second chair leaders is based largely upon trust in the first chair leader.

Trust in The Trenches

What does support look like? Support is not blind obedience. It is the accumulated loyalty extended over time. There are times when loyalty is extended based on past experiences where trust was honored. There have been times in my career when I had extended loyalty and support publicly, even though I may not have agreed when that leader and I discussed things privately. I have been on both sides of that argument as the one exhibiting loyalty and the one receiving loyalty. Or not.

One of the greatest gifts any second chair leader can give their first chair leader is unwavering support. Out of the deep wells of trust developed over the course of time through shared experiences, our endorsement and back-

---

24   *Good to Great*, ibid.

ing exponentially increase. Additionally, our level of belief and trust influences others to share in our trust of that leader as well. Our endorsement garners the trust of others who know us but have no direct knowledge of the first chair leader. The students may not know the senior pastor, but they adore the youth pastor. The youth pastor loves, honors, and fully supports the senior pastor, so the students follow suit. We call that influence. Such is the nature and power of trust earned and trust imputed.

Trust Is Not Blind

UNCHALLENGED LEADERS DO NOT GARNER DEEP TRUST.

Any leader worth their salt or their pay grade does not expect or desire blind trust. Great leaders surround themselves with people who think differently, see things differently, and actively engage in robust conversations around topics where the best outcome we can likely hope for is agreement to disagree. The exchange of ideas and appreciation of different vantage points builds trust. **Unchallenged leaders do not garner deep trust.** Deep trust is earned through contentious, unnerving, and sometimes unpleasant exchanges between colleagues and teammates more committed to the truth than to their pet ideas. The mission is bigger than the mindset.

I was youth pastor at the same church for over fifteen years. We had grown from four students to well over two hundred and fifty students who regularly attended and engaged in our ministries. At some point along the way, we hired a middle school pastor to help lead them while I focused primarily on high school students and their leaders. Emory Waller became my associate, partner, and friend. God helped us, and it was an honor to serve together as a team. Somewhere around the fifteen-year mark, as we were continuing to grow and find favor in our community, I knew in my heart that my time was closing out as the youth pastor at the church we loved. I had always heard that the best time to leave is when you are on top of your game, and nobody wants you to go. I agree with them, but I wish they had forewarned me about how difficult that can be emotionally. My support for my senior pastor, the first chair leader of our church, was going to face its greatest challenge.

I will never forget the meeting. It was Sunday afternoon, and I was summoned to meet alone with my senior pastor. I loved him and supported him unequivocally. I was overjoyed when he accepted the call to lead our church as my first chair leader. During the meeting, my senior pastor intimated he felt strongly that the best way forward for the new youth pastor would be for him to summarily dismiss the current volunteer adult leadership team immediately and without warning. I had built this team from nothing and had strategically and intentionally turned over the reins to virtually every aspect of our student ministry to that group of loyal, faithful, and deeply committed adult and student leaders.

I had always been taught that the true measure of success of a leader is what happens after they leave their post as leader. If the leader leaves and things fall apart, it is proof that the leader has built his own kingdom and failed to empower others to take his place repeatedly over time. He had failed to do the one thing my first senior pastor charged me to do. They had failed to work themselves out of a job. I had worked my entire tenure towards the end goal of working myself out of a job. And now my first chair leader was asking me to blow it all up.

It was incomprehensible for me to understand how this decision was in the best interest of anyone. We argued. I begged him to change his mind. He was convinced that the best strategy would be to ask them all to resign and allow the new youth pastor, a young man I had a relationship with and had even begun to mentor, to choose his own set of leaders. It was likely that he would re-select most of the current leaders, but why put them through this ordeal in the first place? I often wondered if my senior pastor knew that the new youth pastor had confided in me that he also thought it was an unwise plan.

Support Can Be Painful

My senior pastor would not relent, and I chose to support him. I emptied my emotional bank in the meeting, but my arguments did not change the decision of my first chair leader. You may call me old school, but I have also been taught that once a decision has been rendered behind closed doors among the leadership team, it is the job of everyone on the team to support it once we emerge from the meeting. Once the decision is made, I am going to support it even if I don't like it and privately disagree with it. Unless it is immoral or unethical, it is my job to support and defend it as if it were my own idea. My senior pastor knew that about me, but I also reassured him that would be the case in this situation. I was relieved and a bit horrified when he asked me for one final favor.

> I WAS NOWHERE CLOSE TO AGREEMENT WITH HIM. ON THE CONTRARY, I FELT LIKE THIS WAS THE ABSOLUTE WORST THING HE COULD DO.

Once it was clear that he would not relent and would not change his course, my senior pastor asked me to inform the leaders of this decision. My first chair leader asked me to support him and help the leaders on the adult leadership team understand and accept even though I was nowhere close to agreement with him. On the contrary, I felt like this was the absolute worst thing he could do for the new leader rather than the best thing.

I chose to honor him and support him. That evening I called every leader and told them they were going to be dismissed for a period, given a chance to talk with the pastor, and may, later, be asked to serve with the new student pastor. I was not promising them they would be asked to serve again, but I explained to them this was all being done to give the new leader a real chance of surviving as the new leader. Because our leadership team had been so strong and supportive of me, it might be insurmountable unless handled in this way.

I strongly felt we could and would achieve the same goals without the pain of misunderstanding and the hurt of being dismissed. Dismissed seemed a fancy word for firing your volunteers who have done nothing but serve outstandingly and faithfully. It broke my heart, but I did it faithfully and sincerely. I trusted my leader even though I opposed him to his face privately. I supported him publicly and never expressed how I truly felt to my leadership team. I only encouraged them to trust the process and let God be God.

It was one of the hardest things I've ever done, and I pray it was one of the most encouraging in the life of my senior pastor. Unfortunately, he left after about three more years, and the next youth pastor left before he did. Most of those youth workers outlasted both of those guys and stayed well beyond my tenure as well. One of the most powerful ways we can influence others from second chair is to support the person sitting in first chair. Even if it almost kills you at times.

Andy Stanley defines character as the ability to do the right thing, as God defines what is right, even when it hurts.[25] Even when I don't want to. Especially when I don't want to. I did the right thing even though he insisted on making the wrong leadership decision. He believed he was doing the right and best thing for all involved. I did not agree at all and had built my leadership such that when I left, it would not fall apart because it was not built solely around my gifts, abilities, personality, or leadership skills.

I would not share this story with you except that he released me to do so a couple of years later when I asked my former boss to speak at the college I then served as campus pastor. We talked about it that weekend and he, at least partially, agreed with me that it was not the best leadership decision he had ever made. I have opinions about that. But it was best for my church, our students, and our leaders that I support the leader in first chair, although it nearly killed the leader in the second chair emotionally.

One of the great honors and challenges of second chair leadership is the support of the first chair leader.

Even when it hurts.

Personal Reflection and Group Discussion

- How is support different than and like loyalty? How has long-term support and sustained loyalty factored into your tenure as a leader?

- Covey described trust as "the one thing that changes everything." Has this proven to be true in your experience as a leader? Recall instances or seasons where trust was high...and seasons where trust was dreadfully low. What effect did the level of organizational trust have on the culture of the organization or morale of the team?

- Tracy said, "People don't endorse products or people they do not trust. And, once trust is violated, the journey is long, tediously slow, and complicated to rebuild and regain trust." What recommendations would you offer organizations and leaders who are currently experiencing low trust? What are the essential building blocks re-

---

25   Andy Stanley, *Next Generation Leader* (New York: Mulnomah, 2003) 133.

quired to rebuild trust in relationships and teams?

- Have you experienced situations like Tracy's where you were asked to do something that you were convinced was a mistake? What was that internal struggle like for you? How did you handle it? What would you do differently if given the opportunity to do it over?

12

Soloing From Second Chair

Big bands feature a rhythm section, trumpet section, saxophone section, and trombone section. I honestly don't know about the saxophones and trombones, but in the trumpet section, the first chair player is not normally the soloist. First chair players in jazz bands of this size typically are called upon to play high notes…notes well above the top of the normal trumpet range. They are the screamers and screechers, the lead players with iron chops (musical term for lips…or lips of steel in this case). The second chair player is typically the soloist among the four or five trumpeters in the big band trumpet section. It seems a bit counterintuitive.

As second chair leaders, we are given similar authority as we are empowered to envision projects, assemble teams, delegate tasks, plan events, allocate resources, and review the results. Many of these are solo endeavors where we are in charge with little to no input from our first chair counterparts in the organization. We are flying solo and leading the charge within our assigned areas of responsibility and oversight. Like first and second chair trumpeters in big bands, the first chair leads the high notes, but we often are the delegated soloists.

Second Chair Soloing

I learned about this when I was at the governor's honors summer program with my friend, Philip Clark. Philip Clark went on to be a professional orchestral trumpet player in Kansas City for decades. He was the best trumpet player in the state when I was in high school and the best we had at the

University of Georgia when I was in college. I was honored to play beside him, and he always made me sound better than I really was. My best playing days were the days I played in a brass quintet with Phil Clark. He made me better. Imitating his sound, his style, his technique, and his finesse raised me to a whole different level as a trumpet player. When we played in jazz band at Governor's Honors under the direction of Lou Cephas, I thought I would play lead and that he would play solo. I had a slightly higher range and played louder, while he had all the technique and virtuosity. But he sat in first chair for over half the summer... playing the high notes... And I sat in second chair and did my best to play the solos! In the jazz ensemble context, it is normal for the second chair to get the solos even if the first chair leader is better than you!

In the church world, the senior or lead pastor is the first chair leader. In most churches, that person is often the best communicator and the one who does most of the speaking in public. They are the face of the church and the voice of the church. They are, essentially, the soloist. (And, in some cases, they play all the high notes too! Loudly. Sometimes shrilly. But I digress.) In many instances, those of us serving in second chair are often given the privilege and opportunity of preaching in their pulpit on occasion.

As I mentioned previously, my pastor, Tony Vismor, is extremely gracious and generous in allowing those of us on our team with passion and gifting in public speaking to share the preaching opportunities at our church. I probably average preaching two or three times each year and sometimes more. On those occasions, the second chair leader becomes the soloist. I believe we should learn to do so gratefully and graciously. That's what this chapter is about. Soloing from second chair is more art than science.

Practical Tips for Successful Second Chair Soloing

When given the opportunity to "solo" as a second chair leader, there are some things you need to keep in mind. First, see it as an honor and an opportunity. It's a privilege afforded to you by your leader. Don't take it for granted, and certainly don't ever buy the lie that you are entitled to that opportunity. You can lose it just as quickly as you gain it, and rebuilding the trust required to regain the privilege would be painful and painstaking. Be grateful and express your gratitude both privately and publicly.

Next, affirm your leader. Don't be disingenuous, exaggerate or use hyperbole. Sincerely celebrate them and publicly affirm specific things you admire about your leader. If thcy are a great communicator, acknowledge how blessed you all are to enjoy their excellent communication as an organization. If they excel at some point in leadership or teamwork, sincerely and specifically point that out. Celebrate them. Brag on them. It only takes a minute, but it communicates graciousness and gratitude on your behalf and their regard.

Take advantage of the opportunity by preparing early and well. Ask them for input or guidance around topics or issues they might suggest you cover. I often run my ideas by my senior pastor when he asks me to speak on his behalf. But you could take it a step fur-

> ASKING FOR INPUT IS ONE OF THE MOST AFFIRMING STEPS WE CAN TAKE WHEN GIVEN THE OPPORTUNITY TO SOLO AS A SECOND CHEERLEADER.

ther and specifically ask for their opinion and input around the topic or subject you have chosen, as well as pointers on how best to communicate or stories to illustrate. Asking for input is one of the most affirming steps we can take when given the opportunity to solo as a second cheerleader. And, because they know the organization and regularly communicate with the people, they can offer insights and perspectives you might not consider otherwise. Besides, who doesn't like being asked what you think about something you care about?

Share the Mission & Vision

Another step I'll encourage you to take is to tie your message to the mission of your church or organization at some point. Share the vision. Reinforce the slogan. Highlight a value. Communicate how deeply you believe in the mission and clearly express your commitment to your leader and your organization. Tell stories about organizational wins from your area. But don't miss the opportunity to brag about others from outside your realm of influence. Brag on the team. Celebrate what God is doing in and through them.

When you do have the opportunity to raise the flag of your area of responsibility, don't overdo it. Make it specific. Make it clear. Make it compelling.

And give God the ultimate credit. Like my pastor often says, "God is helping us!" Ultimately, testimony and testimonials are ways for us to brag on God and what he is doing in, around, and through us…and often in spite of us. We need to share the mission and vision when given the opportunity on a broader stage, and our people need to hear us voice our belief and buy-in.

Modesty and Appropriateness

Another key step is to honor your limitations and play within the boundaries. Dress appropriately, not extravagantly. Do nothing to draw attention to yourself and away from the message. One of the timeless traditions found in jazz band performances is to simply have the soloist stand while they play. If they are already standing, like players in the trumpet section often tend to be doing, it is common practice for the other players in the section to face the soloist while they are playing. When you are asked to speak or "solo" in the place of your senior leader, it's okay to stand in their stead. But when that time is over, please sit down. If you are given 25 minutes, don't take 30 and don't finish in 15. Either way would draw attention to yourself in a way that could potentially dishonor your leader. Finish before the 25-minute mark.

> DO WHAT WAS EXPECTED OF YOU AND DO IT WELL. DO IT TO THE BEST OF YOUR ABILITIES.

Don't do anything extraordinarily different than the norm without the expressed approval of your leader beforehand. Don't use props or illustrations that work in the student center but may not fly in the main auditorium. Use wisdom and temperance, and common sense. And if you think you might like to include anything unusual or extraordinary, ask a colleague or your boss. Do what was expected of you and do it well. Do it to the best of your abilities. Work at it with humility and grace and gratitude. Stay in your lane, and you will do quite well.

Take A Bow & Sit Down

Our son, Justin, is an accomplished guitarist and singer/songwriter. He regularly plays on a big stage with notable musicians and singers surrounding him. While I am extremely biased and have been privileged to play in bands with some excellent guitarists, Justin is easily my favorite. Like me, Justin is a second chair leader. Though he can lead worship and does so on occasion, he is not the worship leader. He is the guitarist. Most weeks, he plays lead guitar, but some weeks he plays rhythm electric. It all depends on the needs of the song and the prerogative of the worship leader. Justin is a team player who knows his place and takes it seriously.

Like most high school musicians in a rock and roll band, Justin dreamed of making it big in the music business. He fronted several different bands and wrote music in a wide variety of genres. He learned to play guitar in church as our electric guitarist. The music we played required him to learn jazz chords and a variety of musical styles. He took lessons, practiced incessantly, and even completed a bachelor's degree in music for the sole purpose of learning how to play the guitar correctly and understand music more comprehensively. Justin has written tons of songs, recorded albums, and served as a worship team guitarist in notable churches in our region. We are proud of him and his accomplishments. But one thing I find most admirable about our son is the humility he has learned over the years.

Though he is typically confident, he knows who he is and who he is not. He readily recognizes there are other musicians far better than him. But that does not hinder him from becoming the best version of himself he can possibly be. He is the consummate professional musician who practices at home, learns his parts well in advance, shows up early, and never comes to rehearsal unprepared. (I am still learning not to wing it...pros like him know it when I do!) On rare occasions, they will feature him on stage, but most of the time, he is simply satisfied to be a guitar player. Justin knows he *gets* to do this. It is an honor and privilege, not just a job. And it is a responsibility he stewards well. Justin knows when to take a bow and sit down.

Second chair leaders often are thrust into the limelight for a season. For a brief time, the spotlight shines on us, and we are trusted to hold the microphone in the organization. Steward those moments well and you may have future opportunities. Squander them or exploit them, and you may never have the chance again. Know your place. Do your job well. Prepare in advance. Do your homework. Show up early. Be where you are supposed to be before you are supposed to be there. Stay late if necessary. Complement the skills of those around you. Listen to them and play off their riffs. Support them and encourage them continuously. And, when it is over, simply take a courteous bow and sit down.

Similarly, learn from any criticism while not allowing it to crush you. My parents taught me that in any criticism, there is typically at least some grain of truth and something to learn. Look for it and learn from it. Then move on. If you find yourself still celebrating or still lamenting the next day, pray about your thoughts and attitudes or share them with a trusted colleague who will help you keep your mind right and your attitude straight. When the solo is over, sit down. Nod to anyone who applauds. Remember, be gracious and grateful.

One final thought, soon after your solo opportunity, either verbally or in a written note using whatever medium is appropriate to your relationship with your leader, thank them again for the opportunity. One of the highest compliments you'll ever receive is the public endorsement of being asked by the first chair leader to stand in their stead and represent them to your organization. Don't take it lightly. Don't take it for granted. It is not a right; it is a privilege. Every time.

Personal Reflection and Group Discussion

- Soloing from second chair is a metaphor Tracy uses to illustrate times when the first chair allows others in the organization to lead, speak, preach, or serve in some capacity typically reserved as a first-chair function or practice. Have you been given opportunities like this before? How did you feel before, during, and after the opportunity?

- Tracy describes these kinds of opportunities as privileges to be appreciated rather than just rewards we are entitled to enjoy. What dangers might exist if we feel entitled or take them for granted?

- What suggestions might you add to the list Tracy provides in this chapter regarding the stewardship of leading in these opportunities? How can we be gracious and appreciative to our encouragers while remaining supportive of our first-chair leaders?

- Have you ever experienced or observed team cultures where some team members seemed to be vying for positions or grabbing for power? What steps would you recommend to first-chair and second chair leaders to avoid this kind of cultural toxicity? How could they begin to turn around a team fraught with this challenge?

Multiplying From Second Chair

The Great Commission is a multiplicative mission. Jesus oddly chose a handful of somewhat faithful followers as his exit strategy to move the needle of disciple-making from His time through ours. Apparently, they did a good job because two millennia later, we are still here on the planet following Jesus. Now it is our turn to pour the life of Jesus within us into hungry, willing vessels who will do the same within their sphere of influence. It is our calling and life mission to multiply from where we sit in the organization.

Doers and Leaders

In every organization, there are doers and leaders. Doers get things done. They are the go-to men and women called upon when action is imminent and the organization needs to move forward in a positive and productive way. When something needs to be done, they are typically the first ones on the scene and the first ones recruited to the task. They simply put their heads down and get to work to make things better. A vision is a preferred future referring to an unacceptable set of current conditions requiring energy and effort in the here and now to affect the then and there. Every vision needs doers to get it done. Doers move the needle, scratch the surface, and embolden others to join in their activity.

On the other hand, leaders bring others along to do the work more than doing the work themselves. They work through others by helping them discover, develop, and deploy their gifts toward a common goal. Leaders are always on the lookout for someone who could do what they do. Their eyes scan the horizon, continuously searching for potential allies, partners, and future leaders. They look for capacity and character. They see things in others that they may not yet see in themselves. In a sense, they call things that are not as though they already are. Just like Jesus, they see beyond the present state of being into what people could be and should be.

EVERY DOER HAS THE CAPACITY AND THE CALLING TO BECOME A LEADER.

Every organization needs competent doers to accomplish the mission to which they were called. But, beyond all the doing and accomplishment, we are called to foster the development of others while accomplishing the mission. Every doer has the capacity and the calling to become a leader. As followers of Christ, we are called to make disciples who also make disciples. In that sense, Christian doers are to become Christian leaders. However, one of the greatest challenges facing the church involves moving doers to the next level of developing leaders.

Maxwell's Five Levels of Leadership

John Maxwell's widely known five levels of leadership model portrays leadership development as steps on a staircase leading to greater and greater fruitfulness and effectiveness as we move from one level to the next as leaders.[26] The first level only requires the attainment of a position or title. Most titles carry with them a job description describing the responsibilities, to whom they are responsible, and the limits of authority granted that position. When I was first hired at Emmanuel College, I was given the title and rank of an instructor. This gave me the authority to teach in my field of expertise. Every semester, as the posting of final grades got closer and closer, I could exercise the superpower I possessed…granting grades and posting final grades. If a student wanted a certain level of grade, there were hoops through which they had to jump and standards to satisfy before they earned the grade. The only thing standing between them and their final grade was me, the instructor. Final grades were a significant motivator I could use to move my students to action. But, once you have completed my class and received your grade, I no longer have authority and influence in your life as an instructor. I've reached the end of my influence assigned in my job description unless, during the semester, I had earned the right to move to

26 *Developing the Leader Within You*, 5-16.

the second level of leadership with the students entrusted to my care (or you failed the class and were required to take it with me once more)!

Level two leadership moves me from rights and position granted in a job description to the level of permission based on the relationship between the leader and the follower. If, at some point during the semester, a student begins to trust that I care about them as individuals and desire the best for them in our relationship, I have progressed to the second level of leadership, the permission level. Based almost completely on the accumulation of earned trust and respect between the leader and follower, the follower now grants permission for the leader to exert a new level of trust and influence in their lives. A relationship has been forged and fostered to the extent that we know some things about each other and have established some areas of common ground. Somewhere along the way, trust has been granted, and the leadership extends beyond the limits of a job description into other areas of potential influence.

The position level is strictly transactional. You put the effort in and grab the reward on the other side. You jump through the hoops and earn the grade. The tragedy in many organizations lies in the reality that many of their leaders limit the potential of their influence to the level granted by their job description. This is the bare minimum. The job description is only meant to afford us opportunities to foster caring relationships that move beyond the transactions to the transformation of potential within the individuals and, ultimately, within the organization itself. The old maxim proves itself to be true every day, "People don't care how much you know until they know how much you care." Once they know that you care for them sincerely and sacrificially, they will follow, and you will move to the next level. Some experts have mistakenly called these soft skills of leadership, but I submit to you that soft skills are the hardest to master. And, if you don't master them, they will be the lid or limit on your leadership capacity. That's the hard news about soft skills. Trust me on that.

The third level of leadership, according to Maxwell, is the production level. This new level is based on the results we achieve with and through those we lead. Are we moving the ball forward? Is the team winning? Are we making a profit? Are we hitting our goals? Are we becoming more effective and efficient in deliverables? Are we getting better and getting bigger? This one is easier to see because it is measurable. In ministry, we can count the nickels and the noses. Are we more financially solvent and profitable? Do we have more people today than yesterday? Are lives being changed for the better? If so, we are operating as a level three leader with greater influence based on my job performance and effectiveness.

I was fortunate to be a part of a church that, at one point, was growing at the rate of nearly 200 people per year. And as we added another 200 people, we added another staff member to help lead that new group of people and care for their needs. It was easy to see the growth of the organization both in our attendance and the size of our professional team of young pastors. When we began to outgrow our buildings, we brought in modular buildings and began to work on long-term building plans. You could see the tangible results of hard work and the growth of the organization. Only the Lord could see the actual quality and depth of discipleship within the individuals coming to the church. But our leadership gained influence as we continued to flourish in the measurable results. Regardless of the sector you serve in culture, competence is required of you if you're going to continue to advance as a leader. You must be pretty good at something. And others around you must recognize your competence as a valuable addition to your team and organization. We must believe that we are better because you are part of us.

Position, permission, and production are prerequisites to, but not guarantors of, the fourth level of leadership, people development. Am I a better person because you are my leader? Have you invested deeply enough in me that I am now increasing in my own capacity as a follower and a leader? Have you helped me become more than a doer? Am I now leading and continually learning to lead better because of your influence in my life? If you were to leave our organization, would the work continue to thrive and flourish? Would we continue to grow as an organization and as individuals if you were no longer in charge? These are the kinds of indicators regarding the development of people under our care and the multiplication of our leadership through the lives of others. This level takes time. It cannot be microwaved but must be slowly cooked like a meal in a crockpot. When a leader leaves an organization and moves on to another place, the best indicator of the level of their effectiveness will be born out of what happens in the next several weeks, months, and years.

Like level two, this is a bit more squishy or soft. It circles back to the relationships, trust, empowerment, and development within the hearts and lives of those we have served as leaders. It depends on how intentionally and continually we have poured life and leadership into them. Are they better people today because of our influence yesterday? Are they more effective leaders today because they followed (and eventually led with) us yesterday? The ultimate litmus test for our personal leadership is to measure how well those who follow us begin to invest in and empower those who are now following them. In other words, are our followers now leading their own followers to one day become

THE ULTIMATE LITMUS TEST FOR OUR LEADERSHIP IS TO MEASURE HOW WELL THOSE WHO FOLLOW US INVEST IN AND EMPOWER THOSE WHO FOLLOW THEM.

future leaders who will then lead their own future followers to one day become more future leaders who...and on and on? As disciples of Jesus, we are commanded to make disciples of Jesus. However, we are called to take it a step further and make disciples who make disciples who make disciples who make disciples. Over time our leadership moves from simple addition to multiplication and exponential influence. But it takes time, intentionality, and the favor of God.

I believe the fifth of Maxwell's levels is reserved for those serving in the "third third" or final decades of their life course. It is appropriately called the personhood level. This level concerns the personhood of the leader as they have served at all four levels with consistency and persistence over the years and decades. It is the long-term fruit that will remain long after we are gone. It is legacy leadership, and the primary result is respect and honor. These leaders are revered. Trust is implicitly granted. Respect is off the charts. They are almost bigger than life. The best reminder of their fallibility is their own words and spirit of humility. They know that they are not all that. And they are aware of their limits and limitations as people and leaders. There is a surprising level of humility. If they are a follower of Jesus Christ, they are much more aware of their desperation for him at this stage of life than ever before. And they are aware that any positive benefit for those around them was achieved and is being achieved by his grace and mercy. Like a conductor of a renowned symphony orchestra, they pass along the applause to those who played the music as they followed their direction. In my estimation, the best path towards this level of leadership is successful intentional lifelong learning and serving at the other four levels over the long haul. It is, as Eugene Peterson so aptly described, "a long obedience in the same direction."[27]

Leadership Superpower

In many ways, multiplying our leadership is the superpower of leading from the second chair. If a second chair leader is not continually working themselves out of a job, handing off areas of leadership to others, and developing the next generation, they should be relieved of their duties immediately. Other than that, I don't have an opinion!

> IF I AM SATISFIED TO ONLY BE A DOER AS A SECOND CHAIR LEADER, I AM MISSING MY MOST MEANINGFUL POTENTIAL.

Second chair leaders have a greater opportunity to multiply leaders. They have fewer distractions than most first chair leaders. They also have fewer boundaries to overcome. It should be in their job description, and leadership multiplication should be expected of them if not required. If I am satisfied to only be a doer as a second chair leader, I am missing my most meaningful potential and ignoring my primary call to raise up new leaders, strengthen all leaders, and lead leaders. If I do not have an insatiable desire to hand off the baton to the next generation of followers and leaders, it may be time for me to resign my post and step aside from my doing to allow another to lead. The day I no longer want to do that more than anything else is the day I need to retire and get out of the way.

Personal Reflection and Group Discussion

- According to Tracy, what are the differences between doers and leaders? To what extent do you agree or disagree with his delineation of these two roles?

- In your experience, where have you experienced internal resistance to the idea of releasing or relinquishing a task you enjoy or a role

27   Eugene Peterson, *A Long Obedience in the Same Direction* (Downer's Grove: InterVarsity Press, 1980).

you are very gifted in? How have you overcome the temptation to hang on too long in that role? What helps you make those choices?

- Did you find the Maxwell levels of leadership clarifying or helpful? Stop and ponder a few of the key relationships you currently have in your position within the organizations you serve. Do you find yourself at different levels with different individuals or groups? How helpful could it be to know where you stand in the eyes of others at this time?

- Releasing our responsibilities and empowering others requires sensitivity to timing and readiness. What areas do you feel still require your direct oversight or involvement for now? Are there areas where you might need to intentionally begin the process or accelerate the process of hand-off? What next step could you take, and when will you begin?

Second Chair Failure and Fatal Flaws

We all know and can readily recite the public failures of many first chair leaders. Their life is a proverbial fishbowl, and their houses are fashioned from glass. It seems like everyone knows their business, and almost nothing escapes the public eye. Social media provides fuel for hyping their persona and making them seem bigger than life. However, second chair failures are also a prominent part of our cultural reality. Second chair leaders may be spared the front-page headlines regarding their failure, but the devastation and relational debris are no less real.

No one wakes up one morning with a desire to fail. No newlywed couple intends to end their marriage in divorce. No competitive sports team begins the season with a goal of coming in last place. Even though The Peter Principle described the organizational enigma that people in hierarchies tend to "rise to the level of their respective incompetence," their demise was not premeditated or intentional.[28] Yet leaders at every level and in every chair fail every day. This chapter focuses on the potentially fatal flaws of second chair leaders with an eye toward avoiding the pitfalls, habits, and lifestyles that potentially end in leadership failure.

Even on My Best Day

Evil is evil, and sin is sin. In the eyes of God, where we sit on the organizational chart does not provide us any sort of moral advantage, nor does God grade us on the curve. The land at the foot of the cross is leveled. On my

---

28   Lawrence J. Peter, *The Peter Principle* (New York: HarperCollins, 1969).

best day, I sin and fall far short of the glory of God. And that's on my best day. I don't even want to talk about my worst day. My desperation for Jesus and his mercy, compassion, and grace is more obvious to me with each passing year. And my awareness of the implications cascading from the moral failure of leaders regardless of their seat in the organization is amplified, if not terrifying.

> WE ARE ACCOUNTABLE. BUT WE ARE ACCOUNTABLE MORE BECAUSE OF WHERE WE SIT AND WHOM WE SERVE.

How we live matters to God and to others. What we do and what we say matters to God and to others. How we speak and how we treat others matters to God and to others. Second chair leaders are neither above temptation nor beyond the scope of responsibility for our actions, attitudes, words, and intentions. We are accountable. But we are accountable more because of where we sit and whom we serve. There is much at stake. The implications are real. Awareness and preparation are essential. Too much hangs in the balance for us to ignore or lightly approach such a serious issue threatening our very lives and leadership.

Real Accountability

Accountability is not a curse word. Accountability is not something to be avoided like the plague. Accountability does not threaten our position or dampen our capacity to lead. Accountability need not be dreaded but embraced like a dear friend. As a matter of fact, accountability just might save your life and preserve your influence.

Being accountable simply means being responsible to report, explain, and answer to someone else. It is a social construct. Other people must be involved in the process. Effective parents provide accountability for children to follow through on their commitments, tell the truth, do their personal best, and take care of themselves. Teachers hold students accountable for assignments completed, content retention, conceptual understanding, practical application, and skills mastered. Supervisors provide organizational accountability for work completed, quality control, objectives achieved, effectiveness, and efficiency.

In some ways, it seems like we are borrowing this term from the realm of finances. My understanding of finances includes accounts of different natures, including savings accounts, checking accounts, deposits, debits, and balances. Simple math. Maybe, but for a person like me, there's nothing simple about math, and balancing the checkbook has long been the bane of my existence. I can tolerate figuring out our taxes for a few painful days each year, but please don't make me balance the checkbook! Just shoot me.

As we've already discussed, Maxwell's pocket change principle reveals that we leaders inhabit a relational economy whose primary currency is trust—trust we either earn or lose through our daily decisions, attitudes, interactions, and much more. Along with that, the pocket change principle further highlights the dual facts that, first, inside a relational trust-based economy, what's constantly at stake is our credibility; and second, because of that, we leaders must regularly give an accounting to those we lead. There's no way around this—people want to follow a leader they find credible. But to ascribe that credibility to their leader, people also crave *to know*: why we did that, why we said that, what we were thinking when we made that decision, and on and on. Thus, like trust, if we want our credibility intact, we owe people the accountability they reasonably, rightly crave. We owe them access.

But more than mere access, accountability also implies countability. I realize that's not a word, but I think you would agree it's true that trust is measurable or 'count-able.' And the resultant trust or lack thereof is palpable. It's impossible to know exactly how many credibility chips we have in our relational trust accounts at any time, but any reasonably healthy person can have a general sense of whether their chips are up or down. When the chips are up, leadership is easier and more fluid. Resistance is lessened, and momentum seems to rise.

I know that's abstract, but the effect of an abundance of trust or deficit of trust is almost immediately noticeable in our relationships. And that's what's at the heart of accountability. There is much at stake. If it's that important to our leadership as a parent, employee, volunteer, teammate, investor, or friend, why would we ever resist efforts to hold us accountable? I heard it once said that accountability is you holding me responsible for the promises I have made or me holding you accountable for the promises you have made. It is countable, and we are accountable.

Second Chair Fatal Flaws Sampling

So, what are the fatal flaws of second chair leaders? The list that follows is neither complete nor comprehensive. It's really a representative sampling from the collection of overt and covert attitudes and actions that could ultimately take us down or, at the very least, diminish our leadership capacity. And they are not necessarily limited to only second chair leaders.

Most flaws begin insidiously and are hidden beneath the surface. Hardly noticeable, they ripple across the surface of our lives like a rock skipping across the water and barely making a splash. No one else may even notice, but there is a twinge in our spirit and a disturbance in the force of our inner being. It feels a bit slimy, and we are quick to cover it, act as if nothing happened, and pretend it's no big deal, while in our heart of hearts, we know it is wrong. Perhaps we rationalize, explain it away, or dismiss the twinge as no big deal. But the damage is done, and our character is nicked. The veneer of our soul is chipped. And our conscience feels the weight that accompanies loss and moral failure. In that moment, we have an opportunity to reverse the field, admit the failure, accept the responsibility, and allow God to forgive and change us from within. Or not.

In real-time, this can happen in a nanosecond, and the opportunity window is fleeting. Snooze, you lose. Ignore, you snore. Almost no one notices the effect on my moral authority. Nobody sees the dip in my character and fluctuation in my integrity. Oh, there might be a raised eyebrow or two or a gasp as those around us are a bit shocked that we would say such a thing or react in such a way. And, if repeated enough, those gasps become sighs of disappointment as another one bites the dust of moral decline, and our influence diminishes over time.

But I'm being general when we need to be specific. I have been specifically tempted in each of the following ways over my years serving as a second chair leader:

- Envy at the perks and press enjoyed by the first chair.

- Seeming like you do all the work, and they get all the credit.

- The frustration regarding the seeming futility of our marketing schemes, no matter how well conceived or executed, until the first chair publicly endorses the 'product' or initiative.

- The elation by the family gathered in the ICU waiting room when the first chair arrives for a brief visit while nobody seems to notice the vigil you have been keeping with them for hours or days.

- When the ideas you sweat bullets to conceive and strategic plans you meticulously devised are promoted by first chair with no mention of your name or no reference to your efforts.

- When you bust your tail to make the vision of first chair for a project come to pass with creativity and excellence only to have them change their mind and go a different direction at the last minute.

- When no apparent explanation is offered before or after your efforts are ditched.

- When it feels like you are moving all the needles on all the gauges up and to the right, and first chair only notices and comments on the one gauge lagging.

- When first chair entertains a complaint or accusation against you without checking to see if the complainant has approached you directly before lodging their complaint to your boss.

- When someone compliments you after you preach or speak, then compares you to first chair.

As I read over this list, I feel like a terrible human being for allowing myself to feel any of them! The awful truth is that this is only a sampling and not a comprehensive listing. Those are a few examples of opportunities we experience to either grow and allow the Holy Spirit to stretch our capacity of selflessness and compassion or give in to the louder voice screaming inside us to complain, criticize, compare, or keep score.

It's in times like this we need trusted friends or an understanding spouse who recognize and understand the tensions within us and love us enough to hold us to our personal integrity, devotion, loyalty, and commitment to selfless service while denying the need for attention or recognition. At the end of the day, we shouldn't care who gets the credit. And the part of us that does still care who gets the credit needs time with Jesus as he helps us overcome our weakness. When we are at our best, we scarcely even notice such things and can laugh at ourselves and our situations. But on those days when we are weaker and more susceptible, and the enemy perceives an opportunity to hurt us and our organization, we need a handful of friends to help us navigate the treacherous path to honor our moral authority and do the right thing. My best prayer on days like that sounds something like this, "Lord, I want to want what you want."

CHOOSING TO IGNORE WARNING SIGNS IN OUR PERSONAL LIVES IS THE WORST POSSIBLE OPTION.

Choosing to ignore the warning signs and dashboard lights in our personal lives is the worst possible option when it comes to these kinds of temptations or revelations of potential moral weakness. Admitting weakness does not make us weak. Acknowledging feelings can be the start of positive change and potential breakthroughs. I can still hear the words of my youth pastor reminding me that temptation is not sin. It is human. It is a normal part of human existence. It makes you real. Authentic leadership is based on authentic relationships where truth is valued above discomfort, and appropriate honesty is valued above hidden or unclaimed weakness. Owning my emotions and admitting my faults to a couple of trusted friends has been a continual key to any measure of success I have experienced in my life regarding my personal flaws and moral weaknesses.

Wanted: Truth-Tellers

In my experience, there seem to be countless people willing to tell you what you want to hear, but only a handful are willing to be blatantly honest and speak the hard truth when we need trustworthy counsel. Accountability requires people who love Jesus, love me, and love me enough to tell me the truth. The whole truth. I am reminded of the Old Testament account of an alliance between the kings of Israel and Judah as they were contemplating a potential military attack against the king of Aram.[29]

When the Israelite kings initially agreed to combine their forces against Aram, King Jehoshaphat of Judah requested a consultation with the prophets of Israel to discern whether God would support them in their military

---

29   I Kings 22:1-40

initiative. Ahab, king of Israel, polled the 400 prophets of Israel, who all agreed that things would go just fine for their armies and God would give them certain victory. But Jehoshaphat had a sneaking suspicion that the Israelite prophets were less than honest in their recommendation. He asked if there was anyone else considered a reliable prophet in Israel and was referred to the obscure prophet, Micaiah, for a 401st opinion.

At this point, King Ahab confesses that he HATES Micaiah because he never prophesies anything in his favor. Don't you love it when the Bible doesn't sugar-coat the emotions experienced by the people in the narrative? Even the messenger sent to summon Micaiah begged the prophet to go along with the words of the 400 prophets who encouraged the kings to attack the king of Aram. Come on, Micaiah, just tell Ahab what he wants to hear! Micaiah seemed to be playing along with their ploy as he initially agreed with the advice of the other prophets. I can almost hear the sarcasm in his voice! However, when the king pressured Micaiah to tell the whole truth, he changed his tune and predicted the death of King Ahab rather than go along with the false prophecies from the other 400 prophets. Unfortunately, the Israelite kings went against the advice of Micaiah and went to war with Aram anyway. Ahab was killed in battle precisely as the lone prophet had said. Four hundred prophets lied, while one lone prophet courageously spoke the truth. Read that last sentence again. Truth-telling has always been a rare and precious commodity.

While most of our situations are not as dire as that of the kings of Israel, we all need a handful of trusted advisors who love us and our organization enough to consistently speak the cold, hard truth. As second chair leaders, we need a few trusted friends who will speak the truth regardless of what they think we want to hear. Such colleagues are gifts to our leadership. They are courageous and risk our displeasure in the short term rather than conveniently keeping the peace or acquiescing to the peer pressure of those afraid to speak the truth. Their hard truth can keep us out of the ditch and on the right road as we confront our human tendencies and fatal flaws.

Aside from my precious wife, Lisa, I keep a minimum of three such truth-tellers in my closest relationships. They have saved my life, my marriage, and my career on numerous occasions over the years. How about you? Do you have a few trusted friends or colleagues who hold you personally accountable? Do they know your fatal flaws, blind spots, and hidden tendencies? Have you invited them into your life as partners in accountability? Do you regularly consult them, garner their input, listen with an open mind, and take their counsel seriously? If not, why not? If not now, when? It is not too late to admit your need and humbly ask for help. And I love you too much not to tell you the truth.

Personal Reflection and Group Discussion

- Why do you think moral failure is so prevalent in leadership teams today? What safeguards do you and your teams have in place to support each other and provide greater potential for moral success as an organization?

- What areas do you find particularly challenging morally? Someone asked me years ago, "If the enemy were going to take you ought, how would he do it?" How would you respond to that question personally?

- Does anyone else on your team know about your struggles? What suggestions would you offer to young leaders as they try to create safe environments for authenticity and vulnerability? Do you know where you would turn if you were in trouble?

- Tracy lists several potential fatal flaws for second chair leaders. Which of these are potentially challenging for you? What other flaws would you add to the list? What are the keys to giving and receiving genuine accountability for you and your teams?

SECOND CHAIR 15

Second Chair Succession/Legacy

It's your job to work yourself out of a job.

Those were the words spoken to me on my first day on the job as a rookie youth pastor by my wise first chair leader. My mind immediately darted to visions of me standing in the back of the unemployment line! Was he serious?

At the ripe old age of 22 years old, I was very protective of what I thought were my secret skills or the secret sauce to my success. While I was stealing licks from every piano player I ever admired, I would hide my hands so you couldn't see what I was doing. I naively thought that if you knew what I knew, you might become better than me, and there would be no need for me. So, during that season of my life, I refused to share what I had learned with others. I'm embarrassed to admit it, but I was so insecure that giving away trade secrets seemed counterintuitive and certainly counterproductive.

Now fast-forward to my first real full-time church staff position with my first first chair leader telling me that my primary job was to work myself out of a job I had just landed. What in the world did he mean? Before I could even process that statement, my pastor followed up with this one, "If you work yourself out of a job, I will see to it that you always have another one." Little did I know that those words would become my inspiration and personal mantra through every stage of my life to date. My pastor, Larry Timmerman, also told me that day that he didn't care if it took me 25 hours or 65 hours to get my work done each week as long as I got my work done.

Work hard, work smart. The implication was that some people could get all their work done in 25 hours while others of us need a bit more time. Try as I might, I never did find that 25-hour work week!

What does it mean to work yourself out of a job? I believe it means to always be on the lookout for someone who could do what you do. Some people describe the practice as searching for 'eagles' to join our team or surrounding yourself with people smarter than you. That last part comes naturally to me. As leaders, we are perpetually keeping our eyes open and our gaze trained to spot talent, capacity, potential, and hustle. Looking for someone who could do what we do... eventually... potentially. They may not have the skills now, but they have the raw materials within them, just waiting to be cultivated and unleashed to serve a worthy purpose.

Working myself out of a job means that my main job is to multiply. John Maxwell has always thought that followers use addition, but leaders multiply.[30] Find people who could do what you do. Come alongside them and train them in the skills needed. Give them opportunities and safe places to learn how to use those skills. Increasingly give them ownership and empower them to become the decision-makers in those areas. Finally, challenge them to work themselves out of a job while you move on to others as well. We work ourselves out of a job by developing leaders who develop other leaders who develop other leaders who develop other leaders. You get my point.

Pastor Timmerman made a believer out of me. It doesn't matter what you do or where you do it; it is your job as a follower of Jesus and an influencer of people to work yourself out of a job for the sake of this generation and generations to come. Making more and better leaders for the Kingdom of God still motivates me today as a mission worthy of my devotion and life-long energies. Little did I know this idea did not originate with business leadership or military leadership gurus. Its origin is the Bible, and its originator is none other than Jesus Christ himself.

Do for One

In my mind, it's the same strategy Jesus used and commanded us to employ in what we call the Great Commission. The essence of this passage from the Gospel of Matthew instructs us to take initiative as we journey through life

30   *The 21 Irrefutable Laws of Leadership,* 208-210.

as influencers bent on helping others learn to follow God by coming alongside them relationally while assisting in their spiritual growth and personal development. While Jesus didn't challenge us to become messiahs, he did insist we become ser-

WHILE JESUS DIDN'T CHALLENGE US TO BECOME MESSIAHS, HE DID INSIST WE BECOME SERVANTS.

vants. His model of leadership is upside down and counterintuitive in the eyes of most cultures.

Rather than demanding a following, the strategy Jesus followed recognized and responded to the needs of those around Him before offering any advice or spiritual teaching. Content followed compassion. And it seemed as if the content was specifically tailored and nuanced to the situation at hand and the people in the room. Much like a general practitioner physician, time and intention were invested in diagnosing the issues, clarifying the causes, and gaining understanding before offering solutions or prescribing a path forward. In educational settings, it might feel like a shift away from teaching subjects to focusing on students.

Real authority begins in service to God and others – whether those 'others' are inside or outside his family. Such service is characterized by unending love and compassion. When pressed by a theological expert in Jewish law to articulate the highest command of God, Jesus quickly boiled down the hundreds of Jewish laws and ordinances into two simple commands: love God supremely and love others unconditionally.[31] God's style of service embodies meeting people where they are while helping them find their way to where they need to be. Andy Stanley calls it "doing for one what you wish you could do for everyone."[32] Paul reminds the Colossians that "it is Christ in us the hope of glory," mysteriously reminding those around us that there is more to life and a better way to find personal fulfillment and meaning.[33] I have been privileged to enjoy a front-row seat view of this kind of life modeled beautifully by my mother.

My mother, Dottie Reynolds, is 85 years old at the time of this writing. While I make it my goal to have a conversation with her almost every day, it

---

31   Matthew 22:37-39.
32   *Deep and Wide*, 78.
33   Colossians 1:27.

almost requires setting an appointment with her due to her weekly schedule. Mom sings in the church choir on Sundays and rehearses on Wednesdays. After stepping away from the church treasurer role a couple of years ago, she still spends at least one Monday per month counting the offering and preparing the bank deposit. She is the treasurer for one of the local Lions Clubs. She serves on the Barrow Literacy Board of Directors. She handles the books for the clothes closet and assists as a board member of the local food bank. Every week Mom writes checks, makes deposits, pays power bills, funds grocery vouchers, finances fuel vouchers, assists with rent or utilities, and acts as a liaison between local churches helping those in financial crisis through their darkest hours. She helps with the food distribution truck once per month for a half day and assists with semi-monthly blood drives for another half day. She teaches her Sunday School class once per month and attends a weekly two-hour in-depth bible study on Tuesday mornings. Every few weeks, she updates me on the children and adults who have received eyeglasses funded by her Lions Club but disbursed by her to the local vendor. Every year Mom reduces her volunteer load just a little and tells me how she just can't do as much as she used to do!

I am not suggesting we should all be like my mom regarding the sheer volume of service she cheerfully renders each day. Mom is not the first chair leader in any organization she serves, but she leads one of the most exemplary lives of servant leadership I have ever witnessed. She is still working herself out of a job after being professionally retired more than twenty years ago! Do for one what you wish you could do for everyone.

Building Relational Bridges

But it doesn't stop with merely meeting needs and helping people out in a pinch. It requires coming alongside others in our sphere of influence to befriend them, get to know them, and understand them. Our ears must be engaged to listen to their stories and hear their heart before we engage our tongues. We continually build bridges relationally that, hopefully, will one day be strong enough to hold the weight of the Gospel message. Assume that day is not today in most cases. Relational bridges are built on the foundation of listening with our ears and heart.

Earn the right to be heard and develop their trust in you as a friend. Remember, people do not really care how much you know until they know how much you care. Care enough to ask questions and probe their answers to learn their story. Learning their stories is a lot like discovering the why behind what has happened in their lives. Seek first to understand, then to be understood. But be careful not to treat others as a problem to be solved or a riddle to be answered. No one wants to be treated like a project to be completed. As you hear their stories, listen to your heart as it

BE CAREFUL NOT TO TREAT OTHERS AS A PROBLEM TO BE SOLVED OR A RIDDLE TO BE ANSWERED.

softens and connects with their heart to the point that you might feel some of their pain in your heart and empathize with them at some level. Finally, be careful not to categorize or place them in a box. Honor them as unique individuals worthy of respect and dignity. And never stop learning about them and from them. Ever.

Show them that you are for them. Let your encouragement provide oxygen for their soul. Regularly thank them for trusting you with their information and sharing more deeply from their experiences. Affirm their good qualities even if they have a hard time accepting your compliments at first. Go out of your way to take notice of their progress. Catch them being good and affirm such goodness in them. Many people in our world underachieve in life simply because no one has ever expressed confidence in them and their abilities. Be the first to see the positive and call it out. Believe the best about them and for them. And pray for them by name. If they ask you to pray for them, ask if you could pray for them right then and right there. Assure them that your prayer for them right now will greatly increase the likelihood that you will pray for them in the future as well. And don't be surprised if they shed a tear when you call their name in prayer and lift their concerns. It may be the first time that has ever happened to them. Keep it short. Keep it personal. Pray later also. And don't forget to ask them about it when you see them again. Your bridge is growing stronger. But keep on building.

Show Up

Make yourself available and be there for them. Show up. Fight the tendency to make promises you cannot keep and honor any boundaries necessary to keep things healthy and appropriate. But show up at strategic times just to support them. Be with them when you are with them. Be present when you are present with them. But also, be ready to speak when they ask you to give the reason for the hope that you have in your life. When the opportunity arises, share your faith by bragging about what Jesus has done for you in your life experiences. At that point, your words will verify and clarify what your actions have been saying all along. "Love one another as I have loved you. By this will all men know that you are my disciples, by the love you have one for another."[34]

Play to Their Strengths

EVERYONE IN THE ORGANIZATION WINS WHEN WE PLAY TO OUR PERSONAL STRENGTHS AND THE STRENGTHS OF OTHERS ON THE TEAM.

Strengths-based psychology has shown that leaders and followers are most effective and productive when given the opportunity to work from their strengths. Everyone in the organization wins when we play to our personal strengths and the strengths of others on the team. Job satisfaction soars because everyone loves doing something they feel competent and confident in doing. Production increases across the board. The quality of work and standard of excellence is significantly raised as individuals are performing in areas of expertise, creativity, and artistry. Yet, despite supportive research or informal positive observations in support of strengths-based workplaces, not all organizations strive to continually place people in their preferred sweet spots. As second chair leaders, we often have the advantage of facilitating these types of internal cultural changes more readily than our first chair counterparts.

Make it your business to uncover what they do best. Marcus Buckingham defines talent as something people do almost perfectly, seemingly effortlessly, most of the time.[35] Pay attention to where they flourish and where their efforts are excellent. I never cease to be amazed at the next generation and their intellect, capacity, and creative genius. Many of us wrongly assume that if we are naturally adept at something, everyone else is good at it as well. Wrong! Help them recognize their strengths, but also provide opportunities for constant growth and improvement in the areas of their natural gifted-

---

34   John 13:34-35.
35   Marcus Buckingham & Curt Coffman. *First, Break All The Rules* (New York: Simon & Schuster), 71.

ness. One of the best ways to learn is teaching in that area. What if you empowered the gifted young leader to become a teacher or trainer in the area of their talents and abilities? Helping others find their sweet spot is one of the most gratifying roles we fill as second chair leaders. Discovering, developing, and deploying our people in the areas of their greatest strengths is the secret sauce to organizational thriving. Find their strengths and play to them.

Play to Your Strengths

So, when the organization refuses to play to the strengths of its teammates, take it upon yourself to lead the way. Go first and model the behavior for them. Do for yourself what you would like to see done for everyone. Narrow the focus of your life. Fine-tune and focus more and more on what you do best. Do more of what you were made to do. Aspire to only do what only you can do. Increasingly play to your strengths and delegate your weaknesses. Aren't you grateful God made people who love to do what you hate to do? I know I am. One of the most effective ways to begin playing to the strengths of others is to play to your own strengths first.

But what if you are not completely sure where your best strengths lie? Make it your goal to find your sweet spot. One place to begin might be to simply ask others who know you well what you do well. Another approach would be to come at this from the opposite angle and ask others what you do not do well. I must warn you that this can be quite difficult unless you are reasonably secure in your identity. If you are a person of faith, as I am, you might ask God for grace to know the truth about yourself and grace to receive the truth about both your strengths and your weaker areas. Because accurate self-awareness can be tricky, you may be surprised at which areas others perceive you to be stronger or weaker. Assessments like StrengthsFinder 2.0 and the more recent Six Working Geniuses have proven to be invaluable in both my higher education and church work environments.[36][37] Since you are going first in strengths-based work life, you may choose to purchase an assessment online to provide further insights and increased vocabulary around your personal strengths. Regardless of the pathway you choose, find your best strengths, and leverage more time in those areas as you lead the way in your organization.

---

36   Tom Rath. *Strengthsfinder 2.0* (New York: Gallup Press).

37   Patrick M. Lencioni. *The Six Types of Working Genius* (Dallas: Matt Holt Publishing, 2022).

The longer you are with an organization, make sure you are spending more and more of your time working in the zone of your best strengths. While you will never completely avoid working in areas where you are not strong, you can certainly empower more and more people to handle the tasks that you are not proficient in while adding more responsibilities within the scope of your best strengths. Increasingly play to your strengths. And, as you add more and more value to the organization, help your colleagues recognize and understand why you are so energetic about your work and productive with your time. Then encourage others to join you in playing to their best strengths as well.

The Best Version of You

We told our children to become the best version of themselves they could possibly be. We would kiddingly add, "Be yourself; all other selves are taken!" Our tendency in America is to look around us and compare ourselves to those on either side of us. The problem with that approach is that it is based on a philosophy of winners and losers. When we play the comparison game, someone will always come out on the short end of the stick. We will either win or lose every time. A far better approach is to think in terms of completing others rather than competing with others. Everybody wins when we strategically accentuate the positive aspects of our lives by playing to our strengths as a means of completing the team.

Make it your goal to leverage a greater percentage of your life each year towards things that are life-giving for you. Focus more and more of your time and energy each year on areas where you are both effective and fruitful. Once a year, conduct a time audit listing the available hours of each day for a two-week period. Honestly and accurately keep track of what you do each hour of the day during that two-week period. At the end of the two weeks, chart out which hours were invested in areas akin to your strengths. Tabulate both the total hours in the work week and the total hours where you invested your strengths to determine what percentage of your time is currently allotted to working in the areas of your strengths.

Become a river rather than a flood. One of my favorites of Tim Elmore's Habitudes highlights the differences between rivers and floods.[38] This pow-

---

38   Tim Elmore. *Habitudes: The Art of Leading Others* (Atlanta: Growing Leaders, Inc, 2005).

erful image highlights the incredible power of sustained focus. Establish clear boundaries that focus the flow of your energies toward your best gifts and capacities. Do less to accomplish more. Do more of the right things and less of the wrong things. But don't fly solo. Be on constant alert to spot other people who could do what you do. Once spotted, recruit them. Offer them opportunities to join your team. As you expand your team, partner with people who love you enough to tell you the truth, even if it is painful to hear. Consistently garner their insights as you share your insights with them as well. Close your mouth and open your ears. Listen intently to the Holy Spirit and the voices of the few He has placed around you to shape you for His Kingdom work.

Empowering and Multiplying

Empower others. Essentially this means giving them meaningful responsibilities and the authority to carry them forward to completion. As second chair leaders, we have some authority, but it's our job to share that authority as we empower others not only to accomplish tasks but to also make choices and render decisions about issues that matter. Healthy, life-giving leaders empower others continuously and create environments where risk is expected, and initiative is rewarded.

Empowerment requires trust and confidence in the ability of others to do good work and solve problems effectively. It feels risky. And it's typically much easier to play it safe and do it yourself. But if you do that, you will never work yourself out of a job. And remember, it's your job to work yourself out of a job. Someone once told me about the 'four phases of ease,' a simple but effective process for delegation and empowerment. I have used this process hundreds of times in my leadership roles throughout my career.

Phase 1 requires us to do the job in full view of an apprentice. Let them see what you do. Encourage them to ask questions while you provide explanations and rationales behind your processes. You do; they watch. Then we talk about it. According to the complexity of the task or process being modeled, this phase can include several executions of the task as needed.

Phase 2 entails including them in the process and giving them responsibility to help. Now you are sharing the load with them, and they are getting their hands dirty alongside you as you both work together to accomplish the task at hand. This on-the-job training allows for more explanation and questioning as well as gaining experience by doing. It moves from you to us. You both do it. Together.

Phase 3 shifts the responsibility of "doing" over to them while you are available to help if needed. In some cases, you will be needed quite a lot, but in others, you can simply be present while they do the entire process of task completion. Encouragement and sincere praise are key elements of this phase. Use your workspace as a laboratory safe enough for errors and only rescue in case of a pending calamity. Be very careful not to crush the spirit of your protégé in your corrections. No matter how badly they do, find ways to praise them and help them improve. Breathe hopeful encouragement into their soul. This phase may require repetition and sensitivity to the need for instruction or assistance. Let them do the work. Make sure they complete the task. In rare cases, you may have to revisit Phase 2 to boost their confidence and reinforce the steps required to complete the task at hand.

Phase 4 is the culmination of the process where they do everything, and you are there for reference and encouragement. They probably don't need you, but your presence reassures them. Don't rescue them at this point, even if they fail. Let them own their success or failure. Ask them how they felt about it or what they would do differently. Allow them to coach themselves and learn to monitor their own work quality. As they learn and repeatedly succeed, you can move to Phase 5.

Phase 5 is really moving on to someone else while encouraging your protégé or apprentice to begin to work themselves out of a job using the four phases of ease to help another learn how to do what you taught them how to do. You move on but remain available. And you celebrate their success. By the way, nobody said the four phases of ease are easy! Micromanagement or merely dumping assignments on others is much easier. But empowerment, even if messy, is far better. And, if done well, you will indeed work yourself out of a job. And that is your job.

Case Study: Jethro and Moses – Working Yourself Out of a Job

13 The next day Moses took his seat to serve as judge for the people, and they stood around him from morning till evening. 14 When his father-in-law saw all that Moses was doing for the people, he said, "What is this you are doing for the people? Why do you alone sit as judge, while all these people stand around you from morning till evening?"

15 Moses answered him, "Because the people come to me to seek God's will. 16 Whenever they have a dispute, it is brought to me, and I decide between the parties and inform them of God's decrees and instructions."

17 Moses' father-in-law replied, "What you are doing is not good. 18 You and these people who come to you will only wear yourselves out. The work is too heavy for you; you cannot handle it alone. 19 Listen now to me and I will give you some advice, and may God be with you. You must be the people's representative before God and bring their disputes to him. 20 Teach them his decrees and instructions, and show them the way they are to live and how they are to behave. 21 But select capable men from all the people—men who fear God, trustworthy men who hate dishonest gain—and appoint them as officials over thousands, hundreds, fifties, and tens. 22 Have them serve as judges for the people at all times, but have them bring every difficult case to you; the simple cases they can decide themselves. That will make your load lighter, because they will share it with you. 23 If you do this and God so commands, you will be able to stand the strain, and all these people will go home satisfied."

24 Moses listened to his father-in-law and did everything he said. 25 He chose capable men from all Israel and made them leaders of the people, officials over thousands, hundreds, fifties, and tens. 26 They served as judges for the people at all times. The difficult cases they brought to Moses, but the simple ones they decided themselves.

27 Then Moses sent his father-in-law on his way, and Jethro returned to his own country.

Exodus 18:13-27 NIV

Billy Elder was a great father-in-law to me. He was a plumber by trade but was also good at handyman stuff I tend to ignore and regularly miss. He never said it, but I think he was amazed at my lack of knowledge and inattention regarding routine maintenance on everything from changing the oil in my wife's car to replacing air filters on the HVAC units in our house. My

Dad apparently paid other people to do those tasks and failed to mention their importance to me. Or maybe he did, and I was daydreaming. Hard to say. But, when I think of Jethro and his son-in-law, Moses, I am reminded of me and my father-in-law, Billy Elder.

Have you ever considered why Jethro chose to visit Moses in the first place? Call me crazy, but I think I know. Mama was not happy. Not Moses' literal mother, but his wife, Zipporah, was not happy. Moses was never home, and when he was home, he was too tired to play with the kids. And the kids had almost forgotten the face of their father and the sound of his voice. He spent the entirety of every day at the office. And Mama had reached her limits. She had had enough. Follow my logic here. Daddy's little girl was stuck in a dysfunctional marriage, and Jethro found out about it…probably from his wife. So, Jethro was sent as a spy to verify the facts and straighten Moses out. If you read the verses before the text cited above, you will see that Jethro was a wise man who asked good questions and even offered strong words of praise and encouragement before getting down to the real business at hand. That is good psychology and great parenting.

But the next day, Jethro went to the office with Moses. He could not believe what he saw. On the one hand, here was Moses being treated like a guru or supreme court justice. The Israelites brought all their issues to him. And they had a LOT of issues! He barely got his foot inside the door before he was barraged with people complaining about everything from camels to concubines. They all wanted legal advice or court-ordered action to solve their plethora of problems. And the common denominator in all these cases was Moses! Moses apparently had an opinion about everything and thought it was his job to solve every issue and hear every case in the country. Moses couldn't listen fast enough, work long enough, or decide fairly enough to satisfy his customers. They thought they needed more Mo. They were growing increasingly dissatisfied, and Moses was secretly wishing he had ignored the burning bush when he was just a shepherd over his father-in-law's sheep back in the good old days in Midian. Enter Jethro.

On the drive home, Moses was so tired Jethro had to steer the donkey. Utterly exhausted, Moses was in the perfect frame of mind to listen. And Jethro did not hold back. With the same passion he had praised Moses just one day prior, Jethro got right to the point. What you are doing stinks! It is no good. It isn't working and will never work. There is only one of you and hundreds of thousands of them. Moses was working himself into an early grave, and the people were not fans of the system. This is not good. This will never be good. Ever. You cannot handle it alone.

At this point, I am hoping Jethro stopped talking. If he kept right on speaking, as the text seems to indicate, Moses' father-in-law missed a great opportunity for dramatic effect. The pregnant pause. The moment where Moses says something like, "Ok, Captain Obvious, I stink at this and am royally blowing it here. Is that all you've got?" I can just hear the voice of my father-in-law pointing out all the problems and addressing all the obvious wouldas, couldas, and shouldas, then making me beg for solutions. Sadly, the Bible does not include any such dialogue. You cannot handle this alone, Moses. But, I have an idea that could not only save you time but maybe even save your life…and make my daughter happy again.

What follows is some of the most helpful advice ever given to Moses and every other leader since Moses. It is not simply a means of dumping duties on a bunch of other people. It is an empowerment model that military commanders have adopted, government agencies have initiated, companies have employed, and Jesus even borrowed with his disciples. Jethro devised a strategic plan of discovering, developing, and deploying the able-bodied leaders around Moses to do the bulk of the work. The span of care was one person to ten people. It was manageable, replicable, and sustainable. It would scale to fit any sized organization. I call it the Jethro Model. I have used versions of this model of multiplicative empowerment in every role I have played as a second chair leader. I believe it offers wisdom for any age. And it is probably just the plan you need to work yourself out of your job, too.

Work yourself out of a job. Or, at least, make your job manageable, effective, and efficient so you can do your real job while others are empowered to handle all the rest.

And remember, empowerment isn't merely about enhanced organizational functionality.

WORKING YOURSELF OUT OF A JOB IS OFTEN PART OF GOD'S PLAN FOR LEADING SOMEONE ELSE INTO THEIR CALLING.

With the right heart, it's also about loving people and desiring to see those people live into God's fullness for them. For those of us who hope to lead with this bigger picture in mind, working yourself out of a job is often part of God's plan for leading someone else further into their calling. And the organization functions better as that happens.

Personal Reflection and Group Discussion

- Is it really our job to work ourselves out of a job? In what ways do you find this to be true?

- Make a short list of all the things only you can do in your current role. When you compare that list with the other responsibilities in your job description, where might you begin to empower others who could do what you currently do?

- Is it helpful to think in terms of doing for one person what you would love to do for everyone? Does this approach help encourage you to do what you can with what you have currently? How might you instill this kind of thinking in your team?

- What percentage of your time currently is devoted to areas of personal strength in your workplace? What percentage of other team members' time is currently devoted to areas of their strengths? What might be done to help move the needle for each of you so that everyone on your team is working more in their areas of strength? Think about potential next steps, then choose one.

SECOND CHAIR

Second Chair Rewards

16

In my analogy of the band or orchestra, we most often sit in second chair because we weren't good enough to play first chair. We were, at least for the time being, better suited for a lesser position. At some point, you may have challenged the first chair player and lost the challenge. Or, it may have been the decision of the Director as they chose chair placement as their prerogative and, for any number of reasons, decided you were not the person to lead the section. Whether by competition or leadership decision, you were not chosen to sit in that seat.

Therefore, you don't get to play the solos, and you won't be remembered primarily for your virtuous solo artistry. You were given a supporting role. That is not to say your part has less importance or significant value. It's a different role, a different seat on the bus, and a different vantage point. But membership in the second chair family has its rewards and advantages. In this chapter, I want to highlight several of them and celebrate you and your service from wherever you sit in the collective of second chair leaders. But before I do, there is a little-known story from my life I want to share with you since you have journeyed this far into the book with me.

When God Closes One Door…

About twenty years ago, our church dismissed its pastor. While there was not a clear moral failure or scandal, the elders of our church had lost basic trust in their senior pastor to the extent it was time for a change. At the time, I was Campus Pastor at Emmanuel College and part of the School of

Christian Ministries staff of professors. I had served in various roles at our church as a part-time staff member and was the current worship leader at the time of the senior pastoral resignation.

This was not the first time my wife, Lisa, and I had been called upon to help our church through difficult times of pastoral transition. We loved our church and leaned into our commitment to help in any way we could. Due to our longevity and faithfulness to the city and church, our influence would be potentially helpful as we moved into the future as a church community.

Let me plainly state that I have never aspired to be a senior pastor. Student ministry or worship ministry was never a strategic step in a long-term trek toward being a first chair leader in the world of church leadership. But I will never forget the sensation and thought processes I experienced in the wee hours of a Saturday morning during the first few weeks of the transition. I perceive myself to be a pretty good teacher but have never suffered with any delusion that I am an award-winning preacher. However, during this interim period, I had been asked to speak a few times and had developed a different sort of burden for our church than I had ever experienced before or after this season. I doubted seriously that there were many people in the world summoned from their sleep in the middle of the night to invest a few hours of prayer and strategic thought toward the future of my church. I did not interpret that as a divine call, but I knew that if I did not pursue the possibility, I would always wonder and probably regret it. So, I went through the application process and submitted myself to the grueling hoops required for vetting a potential senior pastor.

It was Thanksgiving Eve of that year when I received a phone call from a man who had been one of the elders at the church back in 1983 when Lisa and I first moved to Athens. Dan was the man who volunteered to call me with the news that I had not been selected as the senior pastor. Oddly, as I listened to the pain and hesitation in the voice of my dear friend, all I could think about was how difficult this was for him. I almost hated that I had put him through this! Dan was so gracious and affirming. I believe his greatest fear was hurting me and Lisa to the point we would leave the church. I did my very best to assure him that we had never sensed that this was the definitive will of God for us but that I did not know how else to discern God's guidance than to see the process through. I remember telling Dan that the news stung a little but that we loved our church and would be just fine. I do remember vividly saying something to the effect that if I were not the one chosen, please tell me that our new senior pastor would be Tony Vismor. It was. And twenty years plus later, he still is. I could not be more happy for him…and for us!

Simultaneously with that crazy period of confusion and seeking our next steps, a door of opportunity opened for me with John Maxwell's EQUIP organization to be an Associate Trainer during his Million Leader Mandate. And at Pastor Tony's first elder meeting, he went to the mat for me and secured the funding and permission from the elder board for me to travel to the Philippines twice per year for the next three years to train over 1,500 leaders in metro Manila. To date, I have been to the Philippine Islands over twenty-two times and visited almost every province, training leaders who train other leaders in the church, business sector, and educational venues. None of this would have been possible if I had been the first chair leader. Second chair leadership has its advantages and rewards!

Teamwork Makes the Dream Work

There is nothing quite like being a part of a terrific team. In the sports world, one need not look past college football or other prominent professional team sports to observe the overwhelming desire of elite athletes to use their gifts and talents on elite teams. But great teams are much more than a collection of elite talent. We have watched over and again as lesser-talented teams prove that teamwork is superior to superior talent. One of the most

> GREAT TEAMS ARE MUCH MORE THAN A COLLECTION OF ELITE TALENT.

cherished perks of serving as second chair leader occurs when we are part of a committed, united, well-coached, finely tuned, determined, and disciplined team working alongside each other to accomplish a worthy mission. While there are quite likely strong visionary first chair leaders leading the charge, being an integral part of such a team can be inspiring, invigorating, fulfilling…and fun!

While it all begins with getting the right people on the bus and the right people in the right seats on the bus, the true joy of serving alongside others in a healthy, life-giving environment is almost unparalleled. Such environments and cultures are not accidental or random. They require some key components that are much easier to list than they are to cultivate in any organization. A clear mission or purpose unites and provides the internal impetus necessary for teams to thrive. We must clearly understand what Simon Sinek calls our 'why.'[39]

One of my favorite teams during my tenure in ministry took shape through the 1980s. As a young group of late twenty-somethings, we regularly met to hammer out a mission statement that drove our organization forward in one direction, with a handful of priorities driving our decision-making, calendar-setting, and budget planning. Everybody on the team had an abundance of opinions, and we all saw things from a variety of perspectives. Yet, we stayed the course of heated debates and spirited disagreements required to drill down to the essence of our mission, vision, and values. The final product would fit on the back of a t-shirt, and it was simple enough for an average fourth grader to understand. Our hard work gave us clarity about what we did and why we did it. Having a clear why simplified the process of choosing not only what we were to do each week but also what we were to avoid doing.

IT IS VITAL FOR EVERY TEAM MEMBER TO UNDERSTAND THEIR ROLE AND HOW IT CONTRIBUTES TO THE MISSION OF THE ORGANIZATION.

It is equally vital for every team member to understand their role and how it contributes to the mission of the organization. This is one area where there should be no exceptions. Everyone wants to know that their contribution is important and how it contributes to the success of the team. When I was part of the football camps with Clarke Central High School down at Jekyll Island, GA, each year, I was intrigued by one of Coach Henderson's daily activities. Immediately following supper, after a hard day's work on the field, the offense would line up against the defense and run what they called "perfect plays." I learned that not every play was designed to score a touchdown and that the 'down and distance' factored into the play calling. However, the coaching staff wanted the young players to understand the importance of every block, passing route, stance, position, and the specific role of each player on each play. If they performed the play perfectly and everyone did their part successfully, the premise was that the offense would be unstoppable. The players had to trust the coaches to call the best plays for each situation, but

39   Simon Sinek. *Start With Why* (New York: Penguin Group, 2009).

the coaches had to trust the players to do their job and execute the play as it was called.

Every team member needs to understand their role. Clear job descriptions are vital places to start that process. Everyone needs to know what they are responsible for and who they are responsible or answerable to in every organization. But one more part of developing consistently great teams is achieved by helping clarify what success looks like for everyone on their team. If your parking team or ushers team is successful, what would that look like? Andy Stanley describes the process as "defining the win."[40] What does a win look like for student ministries, worship teams, nursery workers, or children's workers? The team members and leaders of those teams need to take the time and mental energy to hammer out these wins as specifically and simply as possible. Then, each team will need to rehearse this win before every opportunity they have to serve. You may or may not have the time to specifically tie the position to the mission each week, but you must clearly and concisely remind every team member of every team what a win looks like as they serve each day. Great teams do this with consistency.

Solving Problems Together

One other joy of serving as a second chair leader is the satisfaction of solving problems together. You already know my bias toward solving problems at the lowest possible level of the organization, but engaging a group of people to work together on a problem can be exhilarating and rewarding for all involved.

Early in my leadership, I had a fellow band member who loved to claim that he "did not have problems; he had opportunities!" I appreciated his positivity but have found benefit in acknowledging problems or obstacles along the way. Part of the process of solving problems is accurately identifying the problem at hand. Often the problem that presents itself is not the root cause of the problem. It may be merely a symptom of a more significant challenge that, left unchecked, could result in more significant problems down the road. Thus, drilling down a bit deeper to understand the root cause or essential problem is necessary.

Working with a team to properly diagnose, understand, and brainstorm solutions can be satisfying and supremely helpful to the organization. A

40   Andy Stanley, Reggie Joiner & Lane Jones. *7 Practices of Effective Ministry* (Sisters, Oregon: Multnomah Publishers, 2004) 69.

delegated problem to be solved is an opportunity for your team to shine and prove its value. Multiple vantage points can provide a broader understanding and more comprehensive analysis. Troubleshooting in advance can save the organization time, money, and wasted motion in the wrong direction. On the other hand, ignoring or failing to address potential problems in an organization can prove to be devastating. First chair leaders love teams who consistently face the music and learn to dance rather than run away.

ANYBODY CAN SPOT A PROBLEM, BUT IT TAKES A LEADER TO OFFER MEANINGFUL SOLUTIONS.

As a second chair leader, one of the fastest and clearest paths towards increasing your value to the organization is developing the reputation and track record of being an effective problem solver. I have made it a regular practice never to approach my senior leader with a problem before I have formulated a handful of potentially successful solutions as well. **Anybody can spot a problem, but it takes a leader to offer meaningful solutions.** The satisfaction of successfully solving a challenging problem is personally satisfying to me. And first chair leaders are always in pursuit of second chair leaders with a knack for solving tough issues. Furthermore, it is equally rewarding to be considered a trusted confidant and go-to problem solver in the eyes of my first chair leader.

Not Our Cross to Bear

It may seem odd to say this, but the first reward for anyone not seated in the first chair of leadership in any organization is that we do not have to shoulder the burden or carry the ultimate responsibility for the success or failure of the organization. I am not implying that it doesn't matter or that second chair leaders don't care as much as those sitting in first chair. I care deeply and daily feel the weight of responsibility in every organization I have ever served. But if I'm not the principal, the senior pastor, the chief executive, or the president of the college, I will not understand fully the weight that accompanies that role. To be clear, I have served as part of executive teams in almost every organization I have served, and I have empathetically shared the weight and burden of my senior leader. But that is my point exactly.

Part of my reward is sharing the burden and caring enough to be a caregiver alongside my lead leader. When scripture encourages us to bear one another's burdens so that we fulfill the law of Christ, I see the profound privilege we experience by coming alongside those who lead among us to shoulder some of the pain and pressure as if it were our own. But it is much like being a grandparent. We experience the best parts of parenting with our grand-kids, and for brief periods of time, we enjoy the perks of being significant to them and with them, but at the end of the day, we get to take them home. The primary responsibility is not ours. We get some of the perks without the ultimate pressure. This is a double-edged perk in that we have the privilege of knowing part of the ultimate weight of the organization and our first chair leaders on the one side, but on the flip side, we have the advantage of walking away cognizant that the buck really does not stop with us.

Case Study: John the Baptist

One of the clearest examples of this truth found in the Bible inspires us to embrace both who we are and who we are not. John the Baptist, the fore-runner of Jesus, was also his cousin. John was born to a set of older parents, Elizabeth and Zechariah. This sweet couple was unable to have children until God communicated with them through individual angelic visitations and promised that Elizabeth would soon give birth to a son. Further, the angel announced to his parents that this son would fulfill a very important mission in life: he would prepare the way and open the path for the coming Messiah.

We now know that the angel was referring to Jesus, but neither John nor his parents were privy to the name or identity of the coming Messiah. Jesus was born about six months after the birth of John, and their paths would eventually cross in the wilderness when Jesus presented Himself to John for baptism several years later. John was the forerunner who prepared the way for the Messiah, but he was clearly not the Messiah. Jesus would be the first chair leader, not John. John would fulfill a vital role in human history, but he would clearly function as a second chair leader to his first chair leader, Jesus the Messiah. John knew who he was and who he was not.

At that time, John had amassed a huge following and many disciples. Yet, John was always clear regarding his purpose. As people would sincerely ask John if he was the promised Messiah, John would completely deny that and deflect that role to another. He clearly understood that he was simply the voice of one announcing the coming of the Messiah and preparing the way for that specific person. He baptized hundreds in water and preached passionate messages insisting they radically change their hearts and completely reorient their lives to follow God. But he also clearly denied that he was the one who was to come. John knew who he was and who he was not. Yet, the crowds around John and his baptisms continued to grow, and his influence increased exponentially.

When John met Jesus, he both recognized and verbalized to those near him that Jesus was "the Lamb of God who takes away the sin of the world."[41] Even before Jesus approached John to be baptized by him, John acknowledged Jesus as the true Messiah. All his life, he had known this day would come. John may have even daydreamed and wondered just how he would know when the Messiah was there. How would he distinguish the Messiah from all the other faces in the crowd? How could he know for sure? God had apparently spoken to John regarding this moment and assured him that it would be obvious. God would make it clear by giving a sign of confirmation. He would see the Spirit of God descend on the chosen one in the manner of a dove. John would know beyond the shadow of a doubt. And, when Jesus showed up at the Jordan River, God made it abundantly clear. At that moment, with all the zealous pride of a best man announcing a newlywed bride and bridegroom, John introduces Jesus as the long-awaited Messiah.

John was comfortable in his role. He knew who he was and accepted it with gladness. But John also knew his limitations and accepted who he was not. Those of us in second chair positions can learn from John the beauty and power in knowing both your role in the organization and the limitations of that role. Clarity of both concepts provides clear parameters

> **IF WE ARE FULFILLING OUR ROLE YET LONGING FOR ANOTHER, WE WILL NEVER ENJOY OUR JOURNEY.**

around our responsibilities and expectations for us and those around us. Such clarity is a reward in and of itself.

But clarity only satisfies our intellect. We can clearly know our role and execute with excellence while emotionally feeling disconnected or dissatisfied. Only when clarity is paired with humility can we experience the joy of contentment. If we are fulfilling our role yet longing for another, we will never

---

41   John 1:29.

enjoy our journey. John the Baptist knew in his mind that his pronouncement of Jesus as the Messiah would forever change his role in the eyes of his team of followers. Like any second chair leader, John knew that the ascent of his first chair signaled the descent of his own. And with the arrival of Jesus on the scene, what would become of his role as preparer and forerunner? We will continue our case study of John in the conclusion, but for now, we celebrate the rewards of a job well done as an exemplary second chair leader.

Personal Reflection and Group Discussion

- If you serve as a second chair leader, what are some of the benefits you have experienced because of not carrying the weight and responsibilities of first chair? Are there things you can do that you would likely not be able to do otherwise?

- What are some of the things you most enjoy about being part of a team? What are some of the challenges your team is currently facing? Are there any disadvantages to being on your team?

- John the Baptist was clear about who he was and who he was not. Do you currently have clarity around your role and what is expected of you? Similarly, do you know where your limits lie and which decisions are not yours to make? If the answer to either of those questions is no, what can you do very soon to gain clarity about what is expected of you and where your limitations lie?

- Tracy states, "Only when clarity is paired with humility can we experience the joy of contentment. If we are fulfilling our role yet longing for another, we will never enjoy our journey." How content are you with your current role in your organization? As you reflect on your level of contentment, can you identify the sources of your satisfaction or dissatisfaction?

Conclusion: The Magic of Organizational Music-Making

The end goal of any musical performance ensemble, band, choir, orchestra, or jazz band is to make beautiful music. Regardless of the diversity of musical instrumentation, size of the ensemble, genre of music, or level of artistic expertise, the end goal is essentially the same. While aesthetic interpretation and appreciation are as varied and wide as the cultures across the globe, artistic execution, and collaborative musical expression transcend the limitations of time and space as music magically unites us and something truly beautiful occurs. At that moment, no one notices or cares how the seats are arranged or who sits in what seat.

As a student of both music and organizational leadership, I believe there are parallels between the magic of music-making and the magic of organizations working together to accomplish meaningful endeavors. I am calling this *organizational music-making*. While no single analogy fully describes or encompasses the nuance of organizational complexity, the respective roles and relationships inherent in musical ensembles provide many rich parallels and robust examples worthy of our exploration.

In this final chapter, we will endeavor to glean a deeper understanding around a variety of elements inherent in musical performance, performance ensemble dynamics, and the transcendent value of the end goal as it rises far above the positions, seats, and organizational structure. At the end of the day, we all want to make beautiful music.

In My Heart There Rings A Melody

A melody is a succession of notes in rhythm. It is a sequence of notes that is musically satisfying. The melody is typically the most memorable part of a song. It is the part listeners remember and leave singing or humming. Melodic phrases have been compared to sentences in verbal language as they both express a complete thought or idea. Activities like karaoke and games like Name That Tune are based on melodies of popular songs from various cultures. Ironically, not all melodies are equally memorable, and, in fact, some particularly irritating melodic ditties stick in our brains and replay endlessly no matter how hard we try to change the channel of our melodic memory to another station!

I grew up hearing an old Methodist camp-meeting hymn whose lyric, "In my heart there rings a melody of love," is supported by a simple stepwise descending melodic line with a light and playfully bouncy rhythmic accompaniment. Typical of me, I cannot remember more than a smattering of the actual lyrics, but the peppy little tune has weathered more than fifty years of slow fade in my musical memory banks. Ironically, this quirky song lyric contains the essence of the Christian Gospel message, the love of God for us and others.

SONGWRITERS AND ORGANIZATIONAL LEADERS BOTH DESIRE OTHERS TO RECOGNIZE THEIR MELODIES AND WALK AWAY SINGING THEIR TUNE.

Organizational mission statements function much like melodies. The best ones are short and sweet yet somewhat catchy and memorable. In a few words or notes, they explain why we exist. Clear, concise mission statements provide the 'why behind what' regarding organizational strategy, structure, culture, and desired outcomes. When others taste the product, experience the culture, meet the team members, and listen to the melody or mission of the organization, the desired outcome is perfect alignment and resonance between the message and the experience. **Songwriters and organizational leaders both desire others to recognize their melodies and walk away singing their tune.**

I learned in music history classes a concept described as tune borrowing or using borrowed, often more popular, or more widely known melodies to support new words or different harmonic or structural ideas. I was shocked and relieved to learn that many of the Christian hymns from past centuries borrowed popular bar tunes to convey better messages. This is the marketing genius behind using the familiar to introduce the unfamiliar.

One key aspect of borrowed tunes is that you need not employ the entire melodic line but can introduce snippets or musical motifs that touch on the familiar in the minds of the listeners while linking in your message or mission. Much of what we learn and how we learn is caught in this fashion of attaching the unfamiliar to the familiar or building upon the foundation already established.

In organizational music-making, we need our mission articulated repeatedly in the minds and hearts of the people we hope to serve. Our mission must communicate melodically the message that drives our existence and motivates our cause. The right message communicated in the right way is critical.

But there is more to music-making than simple, memorable melodies.

Slightly Out of Tune

To a trained musician, there are few things on the planet more annoying than someone playing or singing out of tune. But what does it mean to be or play out of tune? While my frame of reference is typically musical when it comes to the practice of correct intonation or playing in tune, the concept is also used to describe two or more people who do not agree with or understand each other.

In the world of music, we are referring to someone playing an instrument or singing, not in musical harmony with others. Ironically, it is also possible for an individual to play or sing by themselves and not sing the correct pitches or sing the correct pitches flatly or sharply. My mind immediately recalls countless renderings of the American National Anthem as illustrations of either amazingly accurate intonation or unbelievably bad intonation. They simply do not hit the true pitches and sound dissonant or out of tune.

You have likely attended a live concert where the instrumentalists are warming up on stage, but before the conductor or bandleader begins the concert, someone sounds a pitch, and the others try to match that pitch or tuning note. The sounded pitch becomes the point of reference for all the other players. In orchestras, the instrument is typically the concert or first chair violinist; in bands, it may be the oboe. Jazz bands may tune to the keyboard or piano. In recent years many live performing organizations have taken responsibility for tuning their instruments electronically to the internationally accepted pitch of A440, the musical pitch corresponding to an audio frequency of 440 Hz. You may have observed different instruments moving slides or adjusting their mouthpiece or strings and restriking the note to match the tuning note. While you may not notice if a performer is in tune, you will most likely notice if they are not! And those playing alongside them will most definitely notice.

I believe intonation is critical to organizational leadership as well. While agreement may not relate to the highness or lowness of a note, it most definitely relates to attitudes, working relationships, and organizational culture. When disagreements abound on a large scale, the organization is grossly out of tune. We have certainly experienced the underlying tension of disagreements in the workplace or even in our places of worship. Bad attitudes, rude behavior, gossip, and unhealthy competition for a wide variety of resources hamper the effectiveness and efficiency of many organizations of all shapes and sizes. From sports teams to political parties, we have experienced the shrillness and harshness of people out of tune with their teammates and comrades.

The key to achieving and maintaining good intonation begins with the recognition of the problem. Something or someone is out of tune. Once that is discovered, every effort must be made to correct the problem and restore the correct pitch. The musician or team member must readjust to the agreed-upon standard or retune. Like musicians, people can be quite temperamental and deny the problem or project their intonation issues onto those around them. But, if we are going to become organizational music-makers, we must take the time, invest the energy, and correct the pitch of our relationships, influence, messaging, and communication constantly. Being slightly out of tune must become less acceptable and less frequent.

However, organizational music-making requires more than great melodies and playing in tune.

Imperfect Harmony

When musicians speak of harmony, they are referring to the combination of simultaneously sounded musical notes to produce chords or a progression of chords resulting in a pleasing effect. One of my favorite examples of harmonic variety is the never-ending renditions of Christmas hymns and classic holiday songs we hear once a year for a few months at a time. Just when you think you have heard Silent Night in every way possible, someone changes the chords a bit, and everything but the melody feels different. I love the variety and diversity within the realm of harmony.

At first glance, it might seem that organizational harmony is the same as or very similar to intonation, but I encourage you to look a bit more closely. Dissonance in music is one of the greatest sources of inspiration and beauty ever discovered. Dissonance occurs when there is a sense of tension introduced that needs to be resolved harmonically, plus the journey to its resolution. If you have ever sung a hymn that ended with an 'Amen,' you have experienced short-term tension and release. The dissonance of the suspended fourth scale degree resolved to the consonance of a major third… and everyone felt a tiny bit relieved and content! I see similar parallels in organizations, both large and small.

Not all dissonance or disagreement is bad. Quite the contrary, disagreements and a variety of vantage points force our organizations to explore options and catalyze creative solutions for breakthrough problem-solving. The best teams have a wide variety of back-

> NOT ALL DISSONANCE OR DISAGREEMENT IS BAD.

grounds, perspectives, specialties, and temperaments. When our organizations allow for internal dissonance, honest feedback, and lively discussion, our staff meetings may become more tense and dramatic, but the resolutions and solutions will potentially create long-term harmony because we have allowed short-term tension and release. Ironically, even when the issues are not completely solved, or tensions are not completely resolved, the internal harmony will be richer and more robust as people feel heard and better understood. Learning to agree to disagree and letting others win are critical components to the imperfect harmony of music-making organizations.

However, even more than great melodies, perfect intonation and imperfect harmony are required if our organization is ever to make beautiful music.

Unbalanced Balance

When I am buying concert tickets on the internet for my wife and me, it is commonly my practice to speculate where the sound crew will be in the venue and search for seats as close to them as possible. Before you write me off as a complete lunatic, please allow me a simple explanation. The assumption behind the choice of seats is that the very best sound mix will be in closest proximity to the persons mixing the sound. If the sound technician is less than competent or deaf, all bets are off, however. I probably should not tell you this, but I have only rarely been disappointed though the tickets are a bit more expensive. (By the way, if you really don't care about the sound and just want to be present in the room, why don't you save your money and leave those great seats for folks like me?!?) My assumption is that the sound technician will want to hear all the instruments and want them all to sound as good as possible. In this situation, part of what I am looking for is tonal balance or balance.

The result of tonal balance is the correct distribution of the loudness of each part of the music and the musicians. Have you ever noticed that the trumpets, trombones, and other brass players never sit in the front of the orchestra? There is a reason for that. If the conductor moved the brass or percussion to the front, you would never or rarely ever hear the strings or woodwinds. In addition, have you ever stopped to count the number of violins, violas, cellos, and basses in an orchestra compared to the number of brass players? You would think that the brass players union would protest the ridiculous discrepancies in defense of their poor, outnumbered ranks! But, once again, the goal of these differences is the achievement of the correct distribution of the loudness of each part of the group.

If you have ever attended a concert or musical production primarily to hear your children perform and their part was drowned out by all the others, you understand the need for balance. As a local church musician and youth pastor, I have spent tons of money over my career trying to solve these kinds of issues in live performances so the mamas, daddies, and grandparents will let me keep my job. They came to see…and hear…their kids. I understand that. Even the most musically illiterate person knows whether they can hear their child or not. Similarly, what we need in music and in organizations, is balance.

Organizational leadership tends to live in the tension of unbalanced balance. Balance in any context could refer to any amount, no matter how large or small, that is sufficient to achieve harmony or even distribution. However, balance in an organizational context is more akin to parenting in that it is impossible to consistently distribute time, energy, listening, and attention to every area any more than a parent can accomplish this kind of balance with their children. Situations arise where one area requires more attention and resources than others. Some team members require less time, supervision, instruction, and coaching than others. Giving them more than they need could disrupt the needs in other areas and create resentment for your perceived micro-managing as well. At best, our quest for organizational balance is fluid and often unbalanced.

Paying attention to the right voices at the right time seems to be more art than science. Just as making the number of trumpets exactly equal to the number of violas is both unrealistic and undesirable, the quest for true organizational balance never ends and requires wisdom. The best path forward may be finding peace with an unbalanced balance.

But if we are going to achieve organizational music-making, we still have other considerations.

It Don't Mean a Thing If It Ain't Got That...

All of life emanates rhythm. Rhythm implies systematic arrangement of musical sounds in time and space, particularly as it relates to duration and periodic stress. We might not say it in language that fancy, but we all recognize the beat. Well, at least some of us do. Rhythm builds upon a strong, regular, repeated pattern of movement or sound. Our time is measured in seconds, minutes, hours, days, weeks, and years while divided into days and nights. Athletes, businessmen, and musicians embrace the need for rhythm as a framework and catalyst for effectiveness.

I have long contended that if you can say the first seven letters of the alphabet and count to three, you can do almost anything in music. Almost immediately, I can hear the objectors squawking, "What about 6, 9, 12…or even 4?" Rhythm has traditionally been organized into meters or groupings that tend to build on groups of two beats or three beats. Schooled musicians might call it duple or triple meter, but all of music is arranged around twos and threes. Thus, nine is merely three groups of three with a primary accent on one and secondary pushes on four and seven. But enough of that! The point is that the most infectious part of music to many people is based in rhythm, meter, regularity, and syncopation. Instrumentalists like me sometimes get so lost in the rhythms and grooves of tunes that we are almost unaware that there might be actual lyrics! But what does that have to do with organizational music-making?

THE WRONG MESSAGE AT THE WRONG TIME IS JUST RUDE. THE WRONG MESSAGE AT THE RIGHT TIME IS A MISTAKE. THE RIGHT MESSAGE AT THE WRONG TIME IS AWKWARD. BUT THE RIGHT MESSAGE AT THE RIGHT TIME IS PURE GOLD.

Everything revolves around time and rhythm. The wrong message at the wrong time is just rude. The wrong message at the right time is a mistake. The right message at the wrong time is awkward, premature, or too little too late. But the right message at the right time is pure gold. It can appear brilliant and cutting edge and propel the organization to break through barriers.

What we must also understand is that organizational rhythms are cyclical and repetitive. Great leaders understand that life and leadership encompass seasons, waves, patterns, and regularities. As such, we must learn to ride the waves of success and press into them with hard work. We must instinctively learn to interject change earlier than others think necessary and break the mold before things dissipate or dip adversely. We must marry our mission but date our methods. And we must acknowledge and anticipate the funky and erratic rhythmic syncopations that disrupt our predictable rhythms. They can be the spice of life or the kiss of death.

One often overlooked aspect of rhythm is rest. In musical notation, rests are symbols that mark the absence of a note. Silence is the result. Rests are vital to rhythm in music and in organizations. Knowing when to take a break and how to incorporate regular pauses of activity into our lives and organizations are critical skills required to lead ourselves and others well. Organizations that make beautiful music are continually learning which things to repeat, which habits to ingrain, which actions to continue, which actions to stop or pause, which messages to reiterate, which messages to say again, which messages to never say again, and when to do what or whatever.

Yet, organizational music-making requires more.

Tempos: Moving in Real Time/Just In Time

We live in an economy fixated on speed. Faster is better. Snooze, you lose. Most innovations in technology tout quickness or speed as one of the key selling points in marketing to consumers. All our lives, we have been led to believe that new technologies would make our lives better by handling tasks quicker. From microcomputing to fast food to shipping, we are promised speedy delivery.

In the world of music, tempo is the pace or speed of a piece of music or its performance. For centuries composers have used words to indicate ranges of speed. Allegro indicated a fast pace. Adagio indicates a slower, more deliberate tempo. Andante was middle of the road. The invention of the metronome provided a scientifically precise measurement, beats per minute or BPM. While rhythmic accuracy addresses the need for consistency in pacing and timing, tempo emphasizes the speed of delivery in music. How fast is too fast? How slow is too slow? How do we know when it is just right?

Admittedly, tempo is terribly subjective. Some people like things played fast and frantic. Others prefer slower and more deliberate. Still, others choose a happy medium speed. One is probably not better than the other. Perhaps a better measuring stick would be appropriate tempo or the tempo best suited to the melody, harmony, rhythm, and complexity of the music being performed. Marches tend to be pedantic and regulated. Ballads are preferably more relaxed and flowing. Opening movements of solo sonatas tend to showcase the virtuosity of the soloist and their ability to play quickly, smoothly, or with impressive speed. Tempo depends on the situation at hand. When a composer notates a musical score or a performer records an original song, there is no guarantee that their song will ever be played as it was originally intended after it is released into the world. There is no tempo police hiding behind the curtains to arrest you for speeding or insist you move along at the required minimum speed limit. (In case you are not aware, many state highways and interstates have minimum speeds! My father-in-law is the only person I have ever known to have been stopped on a freeway for going too slow…his daughters never let him live this down!)

Organizational leadership thrives on tempo. One size or speed does not fit all. Larger organizations tend towards complexity, with layers of rules, regulations, and hierarchy creating friction and reducing the overall speed of the organization. Steering a large organization like a government, university, or multinational corporation is akin to turning a cruise ship. Smaller organizations tend to be more nimble, flexible, and built for speed. These smaller, less complex structures handle more like a speedboat. One is not better than the other, but they are different.

Knowing your organization is critical to understanding the best tempo for your team currently. Older, more traditional churches and organizations tend to operate and change at slower tempos than newer church plants. Crisis requires quickened tempos and faster delivery systems. Farms and ranches move slowly but steadily until the storm approaches, or the crops come in, or the herds are in danger. Choosing the correct tempo is a leadership function requiring wisdom, attention, and intention.

Organizational music-making requires constant attention to tempo. Like the world of musical performance, organizational leaders are constantly choosing tempo based on appropriateness for their culture, their team, and their situation.

Melody, intonation, harmony, balance, rhythm, and tempo interdependently contribute to organizational music-making. Only a couple of other considerations remain as we seek to make beautiful music through our respective organizations.

Timbre, Tone & Texture/Culture

All three of these musical constructs relate to tone or quality of sound. Timbre is the perceived sound quality of a musical note or sound as it is produced by a musical instrument or voice. The differences between the sound of a piano and a guitar or tuba and oboe are matters of timbre. Two instruments can play the same note at the same volume level while being perfectly tuned to each other and remain distinct in their unique tone color.

Tone is defined as a steady periodic sound characterized by its pitch, loudness, duration, and timbre. Tones can be pure or straight with no pitch variations or enhanced with a regulated vibrato like a solo violin or operatic tenor.

Texture explores the effect of different layers of sound in music and their interactions. One example would be the traditional rhythm section of a jazz band with piano, guitar, bass, and drums all playing at the same time. Timbre, tone, and texture play an important role in music because they can determine what emotions or feelings are associated with the music as it is played.

I offer these three concepts together as one consideration in music-making because of their independent and interdependent relationships and unique contribution to musical ensembles of all sizes and genres. Just as the fabled single bad apple can spoil the whole bunch of apples or the chain being no stronger than its weakest link, one single instrument with poor tone quality can significantly hamper, if not ruin, the beauty of an ensemble.

When I was in the Redcoat Band at the University of Georgia, my trumpet teacher, Al Ligotti, despised the fall semester each year because of the negative effect on the tone quality of the trumpet players in his symphonic group. For the entire duration of football season, our marching band would be expected to play loudly at the top of or even above the normal trumpet range, causing a bright, over-blown sound to carry over into the wind instrument ensemble. As a career orchestral trumpeter, Mr. Ligotti preferred the dark symphonic tones and timbres rather than the bright marching band tone quality. Our bright sound negatively impacted the desired dark sound of the entire wind ensemble!

I liken timbre, tone, and texture to organizational culture. Culture has been described as the way we do things around our organization. The culture of organizations encompasses values, beliefs, and behaviors that contribute to the unique social and emotional environment. Some organizations have a rigid, hyper-structured environment that functions efficiently but feels uncaring or unconcerned about the individuals within the organization.

> THE WAY WE DO WHAT WE DO AFFECTS WHAT WE DO AND WHAT WE BECOME AS ORGANIZATIONS.

Other organizations are more like a happy-go-lucky band of brothers or sisters who obviously care about each other but can never seem to meet deadlines and fluctuate widely on production and quality control. Our culture becomes the air that we breathe to the extent that we are largely unaware of the perceptions of those outside our organization. We can believe our culture to be one thing while, to an outsider looking in, our culture can feel completely different. The way we do what we do affects what we do and what we become as organizations.

If all I ever see is my organization and my colleagues, my sense of our culture will become myopic and distorted. How we recognize and deal with differences sets the tone of our organization. How we treat each other, speak with each other, and handle our differences affect the tone quality of our tribe. Organizations where people are valued, kindness is consistently applied, opinions are respectfully shared, differences are seriously considered, and trust is highly protected tend to attract people and keep people in their ranks. Organizations that value continuous improvement, personal growth, and team development, as well as organizational mission, vision, and values, tend to thrive over the long term. I believe culture is both caught and taught. It may feel organic and natural to our guests and customers, but the values we esteem must be understood, reinforced, and repeated constantly with our individuals and teams.

Great musicians and great organizations produce beautiful music, in part, because of their timbre, tone, and texture. The instruments are carefully chosen with the resultant sound in mind. The right mixture of people plays at corresponding times for maximum effect. Differences are resolved, rough edges are worked out, and harmony is continuously reinforced. Our musical and corporate cultures are engaging, inviting, and affirming. And at the end of the day, most days, we make beautiful music together.

Now let's put all this together.

Creating Organizational Music-Makers

In case you can't tell by now, I am a fan of leading from second chair. I believe second chair can be one of the best seats in the house. The unique vantage points and seemingly unlimited opportunities to influence continue to intrigue and challenge me even after serving in a variety of organizations as a second chair leader for over four decades.

> "AS A LEADER, IT IS YOUR RESPONSIBILITY TO CREATE AN ENVIRONMENT WHERE PEOPLE ENJOY THEIR WORK AND FIND MEANING IN IT."

I fully agree with Mike Bonem that "second chair leaders who thrive view supervision as an opportunity to coach and develop staff members toward success, even when facing difficult situations."[42] Learning to lead up, lead across, and lead down is highly nuanced, requiring a wide variety of skills and relational competencies. Aside from getting the right people on the team and in the best position to maximize their potential and help the team succeed, second chair leaders must continually create a culture of continu-

---

42   Mike Bonem. *Thriving in the Second Chair* (Nashville: Abingdon Press, 2016) 65.

ous improvement and meaning-making. Clay Scroggins points out that, "As a leader, it is your responsibility to create an environment where people enjoy their work and find meaning in it. You also need to create a team environment where others enjoy working with you. If people enjoy working *with* you, it is much more likely they will potentially enjoy working *for* you."[43]

At the end of the day or the end of a career, others will decide the lasting quality of our work and the success of our leadership. If the end goal is beautiful music, then it truly does not matter what chair you occupy. It matters much more that my contribution was meaningful and contributed to the meaningful music we were striving to produce. Did I play my part with repeated excellence? Did my engagement with my teammates make them better or worse as producers and as people? Did the organization make its best music while I was in charge? Or did we cultivate music-makers at every level of the organization who continue to write better songs, develop stronger skills, appreciate the value of the collective, listen for deeper understanding, communicate with increasing clarity, and build on the foundation of those who went before them? And at the end of the performance, did we deflect the praise and extend the credit to others?

Case Study: John the Baptist Revisited

In the last chapter, we highlighted John the Baptist as an exemplar of what leading from second chair entails. Even before he was born, John's path was clear. His life would serve as the prelude, not the symphony. He would be the entrée, not the main course. He was the opening act, not the headliner. He would be the best man, not the bridegroom. From all biblical accounts, John seemed to clearly understand and embrace his role. However, it is one thing to mentally assent but quite another to live it out. As we reach the conclusion of this book, let's consider how John walked out his second chair assignment.

In John 1, John the Baptist willingly yields positional authority and public recognition over to Jesus, whom he knows is rightly the Lamb of God. As soon as the Father endorses Jesus as the Son "in whom I am well pleased," John yields to the authority of Jesus and confirms Him publicly as the promised Messiah.[44] As another indication of his humility, John balks at the idea

---

43   *How To Lead When You're Not In Charge*, 217.
44   Matthew 3:17.

of baptizing Jesus until Jesus insists it is the right way forward. Further, in the time leading up to the arrival of the Messiah, John consistently referred to himself as unworthy even to lace the sandals of the future king. The reality that John never attempts to steal the crown or the title he knew was not his to carry is further evidence of his submissive spirit and selfless devotion. He knew his seat was second chair and never sought an upgrade.

However, nothing could prepare John for the days following the baptism of Jesus when his followers quickly began to desert him and follow the newly acclaimed leader. In John 3, one of John's disciples points out the obvious attrition of their team and draws attention to the reality that Jesus is growing in popularity, and everyone seems to be choosing to follow Him rather than John. It is surprising that Scripture gives no indication of the internal emotional struggle John surely experienced, as many of his closest associates abandoned him for Jesus. On the contrary, John clearly underscores the necessity of this arrangement, asserting, "He must increase, but I must decrease."[45]

While little is known about the specifics of the ministry of John the Baptist after this time, we know that for a brief season, his ministry continued though its scope and magnitude were greatly diminished. At the height of Jesus' ministry, John was seized by King Herod and thrown into prison for his boldness in confronting the king's adulterous lifestyle. John's life and influence radically changed. Times were dark, and life was uncertain. I doubt that John had any idea his season of decrease would reach such depths.

Things got so bad for John that he doubted both himself and the bold declarations he made regarding Jesus at His baptism in the desert just months before. Jesus was nothing like the leader John had anticipated or expected as a Messiah. Rather than being ruthless and demanding, Jesus was compassionate and humble. He performed amazing signs, wonders, and healings. John heard rumors that even dead people were raised to life. Social outcasts were radically changed. But the oppressive Roman rule seemed to grow stronger while the Jewish leaders had little regard for Jesus as a teacher, prophet, or priest – much less a king or messiah!

Amid those doubts, John sent a friend to ask Jesus for confirmation as to whether He was, indeed, the Messiah. Yet, Jesus did not chide John nor rebuke him for his crisis of belief. He simply pointed to his accomplish-

---

45   John 3:30.

ments and the life transformations that continually surrounded him as he encountered people each day. But, after John's messenger departed, Jesus publicly acclaimed John the Baptist as a man like no other before or after him. And not long afterward, John gave the ultimate sacrifice. He was beheaded for speaking the truth and remaining faithful to his role as second chair to the Messiah. What likely seemed an abject failure in the eyes of the world was the highest honor and ultimate achievement for the forerunner of Jesus Christ.

And that's it. Curtains close on John the Baptist.

Through it all, he resisted the intoxicating upward pull of pride, self-elevation, and competition to stay seated in the chair to which he knew he was called. The Second Chair. And in this chair—in the tireless and faithful life spent yielding to things more important than himself—the beautiful music of Jesus's Kingdom was made audible and known through him. John 10:42 tells us as much as it concludes with this final observation:

"*And in that place,*"— the place where John the Baptist had served from his second chair, that is— "*many believed in Jesus.*"[46]

The lifesaving melody of Jesus's gospel could be heard, in part, because John the Baptist wanted so much for others to hear it that he joyfully made less of himself than perhaps he could have.

Should we not all be the same?

If the goal is making beautiful music—whether in our organizations or in the Kingdom harvest fields— should we not aspire to a life-like John the Baptist's? A life spent yielding our personal ambition to solo and to shine in the eyes of others so that we can instead learn to rest comfortably and serve passionately from a chair that embraces hiddenness as the path to fullness, being made less as preferable to being made more, and seating oneself last as the way to finding oneself first.

May God grant us the grace and persistence to faithfully serve from our respective chair to the very best of our capacity as followers who simply went before. And may we be eternally grateful for the honor and privilege of occupying the honored seat of second chair leader.

---

46   John 10:40-42.

Personal Reflection and Group Discussion

- What kind of music is your organization making? Is there a clearly articulated theme or mission driving the structure and organization, or are there competing melodies vying for dominance or attention?

- Is there a culture of concord or dissonance? Are individuals and teams involved in civil discourse or unkind rhetoric? When a voice or group of players gets out of tune or out of balance, is there space and latitude to correct, learn, grow, and change?

- How well do team members recognize their roles, embrace the vision, and engage with one another in pursuit of the success of the organization? For the most part, are people sitting in the right seats on the bus? How well are the sections or departments aligned, staying in their lane, and celebrating the other departments and individuals?

- John the Baptist securely and humbly stated, "He must increase, I must decrease." As you reflect on that statement and consider your seat in your organization, how comfortable are you with the idea of someone else taking your place or receiving the bulk of the credit for the work you have done?

About the Author

Dr. C. Tracy Reynolds: With over forty years in pastoral ministry, Tracy has served in multiple capacities within the church, as a college professor, a VP in higher education, and as an associate trainer for John Maxwell's EQUIP. He is a lifelong learner in leadership, discipleship, and organizational development. Tracy currently serves at Grace Fellowship in Watkinsville, GA, and co-hosts Next Step Leadership, a podcast with Chris Maxwell.
He and his wife, Lisa, have been married for over forty years. They have two grown children and three granddaughters. He loves jazz, coffee, Braves baseball, and spending time with the tiny people that call him "Papa."

On-Line handles:
Website address: https://www.ctracyreynolds.com
Facebook: ctracyreynoldsauthor
Twitter: @ctracyreynolds
LinkedIn: Tracy Reynolds
Email: ctracyreynolds@gmail.com

SECOND CHAIR LEADERSHIP

ONLINE RESOURCES

Scan the FlowCode below to access exclusive online resources at

https://www.ctracyreynolds.com/

Printed in the USA
CPSIA information can be obtained
at www.ICGtesting.com
LVHW021948061224
798427LV00049B/1634

* 9 7 8 1 9 6 0 0 2 4 0 8 4 *